COMBAT AIRCRAFT S

CW00407373

B-52
Stratofortress

LINDSAY PEACOCK

OSPREY PUBLISHING LONDON

Published in 1987 by
Osprey Publishing Ltd
Member Company of the George Philip Group
12–14 Long Acre, London WC2E 9LP

This book is copyrighted under the Berne Convention.
All rights reserved. Apart from any fair dealing for the
purpose of private study, research, criticism or review,
as permitted under the Copyright Act, 1956, no part
of this publication may be reproduced, stored in a
retrieval system, or transmitted in any form or by any
means, electronic, electrical, chemical, mechanical,
optical, photocopying, recording or otherwise, without
the prior permission of copyright owner. Enquiries
should be addressed to the Publishers.

© Copyright 1987 Bedford Editions Ltd.

British Library Cataloguing in Publication Data

Peacock, Lindsay T.
    Boeing B-52.–(Osprey combat aircraft)
    1. B-52 Bomber–History
    I. Title
    623.74'63   UG1242.B6

ISBN 0-85045-749-1

Typeset by Flair plan Photo-typesetting Ltd.
Printed by Proost International Book Production,
Turnhout, Belgium.

Designed by Little Oak Studios
Colour artworks: Mike Keep
Cutaway drawing: © Pilot Press Ltd.
Photographs: The publishers thank The Boeing Company
and the United States Department of Defense for
supplying the photographs reproduced in this book.

The Author
LINDSAY PEACOCK is an aviation journalist and
photographer who has written extensively on military
aircraft subjects for books and magazines, especially in
areas of specific interest to aircraft modellers. He has
travelled widely in pursuit of his profession and hobbies,
and spent much time at military aircraft establishments
observing his subjects at close quarters. His other books in
this series are *F/A-18 Hornet*, *F-14 Tomcat*, *B-1B* and the
forthcoming *AH-1 HueyCobra*.

Contents

1

Genesis of the Stratofortress

B Y THE late 1940s, Boeing's reputation as a manufacturer of heavy bombers was well-nigh unassailable, despite the fact that it was based largely on just two designs, both of which had been blooded in combat in two very different theatres during the course of World War II. The exploits of the B-17 Flying Fortress in Europe are legion and need no recounting here, while the later and larger B-29 Superfortress had been instrumental in carrying the war to the Japanese homeland, eventually gaining immortality when "Enola Gay" released the first nuclear device to be used in anger, over Hiroshima in August 1945.

Not content to rest on its laurels, Boeing's design team then conceived the B-47 Stratojet, a type which provided Strategic Air Command with its first truly effective jet bomber and one that laid the foundations for the company's remarkable post-war success story. Eventually produced in vast numbers, the B-47

was, nevertheless, still very much an unknown quantity when, in early 1946, the US Army Air Force drew up a requirement for a second generation heavy bomber possessing an intercontinental range capability to replace the Convair B-36 which, of course, had still to enter service.

With such a lucrative project in the offing, Boeing was naturally keen to get "a slice of the action" and wasted little time in initiating design work. However, since the company had still to learn just how good the B-47 really was, it was hardly suprising that early proposals envisaged the use of turboprop propulsion, there still being more than a little suspicion surrounding the new-fangled turbojet engines. In consequence, it took two years' work and more than

Below: While assigned to the Air Research and Development Command's Proving Ground facility at Eglin AFB in Florida, RB-52B 2012 took time out from more pressing duties to pose with an example of the type it replaced, Convair's B-36.

Above: The first of the eventual total of 744 examples of the Boeing Stratofortress to take to the air was the YB-52, which made its maiden flight from Seattle on 15 April 1952.

30 different design studies utilising varying combinations of engine, wing and gross weight before Boeing reluctantly reached the conclusion that turboprop power was not the way to go.

By then, of course, the XB-47 had flown and test data generated by early flights was beginning to provide clear evidence that significant performance gains could be had by utilising jet engines in conjunction with an aerodynamically "clean" structure. Even then, it was to take some months before, over a lunch-time meeting in late October 1948, despairing of ever making satisfactory progress with the turboprop concept, the USAF's chief of bomber development, Colonel Henry Warden, suggested that senior Boeing design staff direct their energies towards preparing a proposal based on the use of the Pratt & Whitney J57 turbojet engine, itself then in the early developmental stage.

In retrospect, it seems that this suggestion arose more out of a sense of desperation than anything else but, like many of history's accidents, it proved to be an inspired act. On the following morning, after a period of intense "brain-storming", Boeing engineers were back in touch with Warden to inform him that they would produce a firm proposal just 72 hours later. What evolved in a frantic weekend in Dayton's Van Cleve hotel was the Boeing Model 464-49-0, this basically being an eight-engined bomber in the 330,000lb (150,000kg) weight category, capable of toting a 10,000lb (4,500kg) bomb load some 8,000 miles (12,875km) and with an estimated maximum speed of 572mph (920km/h). Other features of the design were 35 degrees of wing sweep, podded engines as on the XB-47 and bicycle main undercarriage members with outrigger wheels for stability, again bearing a distinct resemblance to that employed on the much smaller Stratojet.

Hardly surprisingly, in view of the hurried nature of the work undertaken in Ohio, some refinement of the initial proposal occurred as the design was firmed up. Nevertheless, the basic shape was remarkably similar to the aircraft which emerged from Boeing's factory at Seattle in late November 1951.

Air Force resistance

At the same time as the Boeing team was engaged in its frenetic activity in Dayton, another key character in the B-52 saga was settling into his new appointment as the Commanding General of Strategic Air Command. The stuff of legend, Lieutenant General Curtis E. LeMay quickly recognised the potential of Boeing's design but, even with his not inconsiderable weight behind it, the B-52 still encountered more than a little resistance within the Air Force organisation.

Some of this resistance arose out of the fact that the aircraft represented a quantum leap in several areas of technology, while some were concerned with the impact it would have on the budget. It was already evident that existing support facilities would be inadequate, and vast sums of money would have to be spent on construction projects at bases selected to support operational B-52 units.

All this came when the United States had only recently concluded involvement in a major conflict and there was understandable resistance to matters of a military nature, many people being content just to enjoy the peace. Soon, of course, the USA became embroiled in the Korean War in the summer of 1950, but this conflict was fortuitous in so far as the B-52 was concerned for it opened up the funding flood-gates, Boeing's bomber getting its fair share of the huge amounts of money spent on all areas of defence during the following few years.

In the meantime, the new bomber had first to be built and then negotiate the hurdle of flight testing before it could enter operational service with SAC. Construction of the two prototypes—XB-52 49-230 and YB-52 49-231, the latter differing only in that it was instrumented for flutter tests—began using funding set aside in Fiscal Year 1949 and was undertaken at Seattle. It was a lengthy process: unlike the B-47 which relied as far as was possible on well-proven equipment, the B-52 incorporated many innovative features and sub-systems.

By autumn 1951, the XB-52 was nearing completion in the huge assembly hall at Seattle but such was the degree of secrecy which surrounded this project

Below: Laden with a clutch of 24 M117 750lb bombs underwing (and with a further 27 housed internally), B-52F 70147 sets off from Andersen AFB, Guam on the long haul to Vietnam. It was this model which first entered combat, on 18 June 1965.

that the roll-out ceremony—if one can use that term to describe what was essentially a non-event—was accomplished under cover of darkness on the night of 29 November 1951. Quite extraordinary security measures were taken to prevent prying eyes obtaining a glimpse of this aircraft, the entire airframe being shrouded in tarpaulin for the short journey to the flight test hangar where it was to undergo a lengthy series of system checks and taxi trials which should have culminated in a maiden flight.

Maiden flight

Unfortunately, a disastrous failure during final check of the pneumatic system resulted in considerable damage to the wing trailing edge. This necessitated the XB-52's return to the assembly hall for repair work and it therefore fell to the YB-52 to make the maiden flight, an event which took place on 15 April 1952 when Boeing test pilot A. M. "Tex" Johnson and USAF test pilot Lt. Col. Guy M. Town-

send clambered aboard and completed the short trip from Boeing Field in Seattle to Moses Lakes where this aircraft was briefly based while flight evaluation got under way. In due course, the XB-52 also joined the test programme, making its first flight on 2 October 1952. These two prototypes bore the brunt of development until 5 August 1954 when the first of three B-52As (52-001) took to the air.

By that time, of course, General LeMay had truly won his battle for the B-52, some 50 B/RB-52Bs and 35 B-52Cs being on order at a cost approaching the $1 billion mark and little more than a month was to elapse before a further $227 million was set aside for the procurement of an initial batch of 50 B-52Ds. Clearly, Boeing's Stratofortress had every prospect of assuming the mantle of being SAC's "big stick" from the Convair B-36.

Below: Fitting the massive fin to the Stratofortress was always a tricky operation, but was made slightly easier by the use of a mobile crane device installed in the assembly halls at Wichita and Seattle. Here, engineers check that it is seated correctly.

2

Stratofortress Technical Features

ALTHOUGH it now looks rather dated in comparison with more modern bombers such as Rockwell's B-1B, when the B-52 made its debut it was in the very vanguard of aeronautical progress, incorporating much that was new and unproven. At first glance, though, one might be excused for concluding that it was in essence merely a logical "growth" of the B-47, for it certainly made use of lessons learned by Boeing in bringing the Stratojet from the status of a promising project to that of an operational system. Such a conclusion would, however, be rather wide of the mark, the B-52 making a number of significant contributions to the Boeing success story of the late 1950s and early 1960s when the 707 commercial jet transport led the way in revolutionising air travel for the masses.

A classic instance of this is provided by the wing which, despite its massive size—it has an area of no less than 4,000sq ft (371m^2)—employed very different design criteria. This permitted a much lighter structure which, in turn, bestowed a number of important benefits. Obviously, it resulted in a much lighter airframe than would otherwise have been possible, although when one considers that later models of the Stratofortress tipped the scales at around 488,000lb (221,351kg), "lightness" is perhaps not quite the right word to use when discussing the B-52.

Also, unlike that of the B-47, the wing could be used to accommodate fuel, and this was of great importance in achieving the desired unrefuelled intercontinental range capability. Another advantage which held promise for future designs was that the

Below: Adopted when the B-52D model assumed responsibility for "Arc Light" conventional bombing missions over Vietnam, the black and camouflage finish gave this variant a most sinister appearance. No other B-52 was painted in this way.

BOEING B-52G STRATOFORTRESS CUTAWAY DRAWING KEY

1. Nose radome.
2. ALT 28 ECM antenna.
3. Electronic countermeasures (ECM) equipment bay.
4. Front pressure bulkhead.
5. Electronics cooling air intake
6. Bombing radar
7. Low-light television scanner turret (EVS system), infra-red on starboard side.
8. Television camera unit.
9. ALQ 117 radar warning antenna.
10. Underfloor control runs.
11. Control column.
12. Rudder pedals.
13. Windscreen wipers.
14. Instrument panel shroud.
15. Windscreen panels
16. Cockpit eyebrow windows.
17. Cockpit roof escape/ ejection hatches.
18. Co-pilot's ejection seat.
19. Drogue chute container
20. Pilot's ejection seat.
21. Flight deck floor level.
22. Navigator's instrument console.
23. Ventral escape/ejection hatch, port and starboard.
24. Radar navigator's downward ejection seat, navigator to starboard.
25. Access ladder and hatch to flight deck.
26. EWO instructor's folding seat.
27. Electronics equipment rack.
28. In-flight refuelling receptacle, open.
29. Refuelling delivery line.
30. Electronic warfare officer's (EWO) ejection seat.
31. Rear crew members escape/ ejection hatches.
32. EWO's instrument panel.
33. Gunner's remote control panel.
34. Gunner's ejection seat.
35. Navigation instructor's folding seat.
36. Radio and electronics racks.
37. Ventral entry hatch and ladder.
38. Lower deck rear pressure bulkhead.
39. ECM aerials.
40. ECM equipment bay.
41. Cooling air ducting.
42. Upper deck rear pressure bulkhead.
43. Water injection tank, capacity 1,200 US gal (4 542 l).
44. Fuselage upper longeron.
45. Astro navigation antenna.
46. Tank access hatches.
47. Leading edge 'strakelets' fitted to identify cruise missile carriers.
48. Forward fuselage fuel tank.
49. Air conditioning plant.
50. Forward starboard main undercarriage bogie.
51. Landing lamp.

52. Forward port main undercarriage bogie.
53. Torque scissor links.
54. Steering jacks.
55. Main undercarriage door.
56. Main undercarriage leg strut.
57. Wing front spar/fuselage/ main undercarriage attachment frame.
58. Main undercarriage wheel bay.
59. Doppler aerial.
60. Central electronic equipment bay.
61. Air conditioning intake duct.
62. Front spar attachment joint.
63. Wing root rib.
64. Wing panel bolted attachment joint.
65. Centre section fuel tank bay.
66. Wing centre section carry- through.
67. Starboard wing attachment joint.
68. Vortex generators.
69. Starboard wing integral fuel tank bays; total fuel system capacity (includes external tanks) 48,030 US gal (181,813 l).
70. Engine ignition control unit.
71. Bleed air ducting.
72. Starboard engine nacelles.
73. Nacelle pylons.
74. Fixed external fuel tank, capacity 700 US gal (2,650 l).
75. Tank pylon.
76. Fuel venting channels.
77. Tip surge tank.
78. Starboard navigation light.
79. Wing tip fairing.
80. Fixed portion of trailing edge.
81. Starboard outrigger wheel, stowed position.
82. Hydraulic equipment bay.
83. Roll control spoiler panels, open.
84. Outboard single-slotted, Fowler-type flap, down position.
85. Inboard fixed trailing edge segment.

86. Chaff dispensers and flare launchers.
87. Inboard single slotted flap, down position.
88. Flap guide rails.
89. Flap screw jacks.
90. Flap drive torque shaft.
91. Life raft stowage.
92. Wing centre section/ longeron ties.
93. Central flap drive motor.
94. Rear spar attachment joint.
95. AGM-69 missile environmental control unit.
96. Bomb bay rotary missile launcher.
97. AGM-69 SRAM air to ground missiles.
98. Bomb bay rear bulkhead.
99. Rear fuselage bag-type fuel tanks.
100. Rear fuselage longeron.
101. Fuel delivery and transfer piping.
102. Fuselage skin panelling.
103. Fuselage fuel system surge tank.
104. Data link antenna.
105. Rear fuselage frame construction.

106. Rear equipment bay air conditioning plant.
107. Ram air intake.
108. Starboard tailplane.
109. Vortex generators.
110. Starboard elevator.
111. Fin spar attachment joint: fin folds to starboard.
112. Tailfin rib construction.
113. VOR aerial.
114. Lightning isolator.
115. Fin tip aerial fairing.
116. Rudder.
117. Rudder tab.
118. Hydraulic rudder control jack.
119. Rudder aerodynamic balance.
120. Rear ECM and fire control electronics pack.
121. ECM aerial fairing.
122. Brake parachute stowage.
123. Parachute and door release mechanism.
124. ALQ-117 retractable aerial fairing.
125. AN/ASG-15 search radome.
126. ALQ-117 and APR-25 ECM radome.

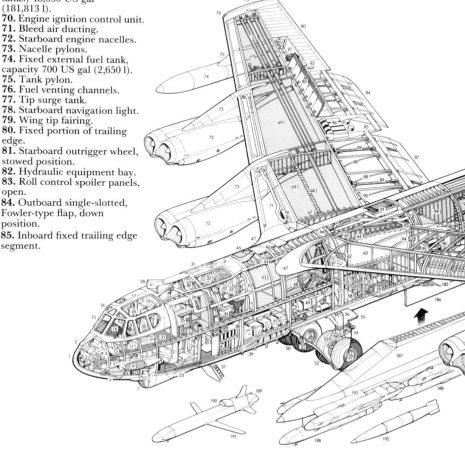

127. Four 0.5-in (12.7mm) machine guns.
128. AN/ASG-15 tracking radome.
129. Remote control gun turret.
130. Ammunition feed chutes.
131. Ammunition tanks, 600 rounds per gun.
132. Elevator tab.
133. Port elevator.
134. ALQ-153 tail warning radar.
135. All-moving tailplane construction.
136. Tailplane carry-through box section spar.
137. Elevator aerodynamic balance.
138. Centre section sealing plate.
139. Tailplane trimming screw jack.
140. Air conditioning ducting.
141. Fuel system venting pipes.
142. Ventral access hatch.
143. Rear fuselage ECM equipment bay.
144. ECM aerials.
145. Strike camera compartment.
146. Rear main undercarriage wheel bay.
147. Bomb/wheel bay box section longeron.

148. Main undercarriage mounting frame.
149. Hydraulic retraction jack.
150. Rear main undercarriage bogie units.
151. Flap shroud ribs.
152. ECM aerials.
153. Fixed portion of trailing edge.
154. Port flaps, down position.
155. Outboard single slotted flap.
156. Port roll control spoiler panels.
157. Hydraulic reservoir.
158. Outrigger wheel bay.
159. Fixed portion of trailing edge.
160. Glass-fibre wing tip fairing.
161. Port navigation light.
162. Outer wing panel integral fuel tank.

163. Port outrigger wheel.
164. Fixed external fuel tank.
165. Fuel tank pylon.
166. Outrigger wheel retraction strut.
167. Outer wing panel attachment joint.
168. Engine pylon mounting rib.
169. Pylon rear attachment strut.
170. Engine pylon construction.
171. Pratt & Whitney J57-P-43WB turbojet engine.
172. Engine oil tank, capacity 8.5 US gal (32 l).
173. Accessory equipment gearbox.
174. Generator cooling air duct.
175. Oil cooler ram air intakes.
176. Engine air intakes.
177. Detachable cowling panels.

178. Leading edge rib construction.
179. Front spar.
180. Wing rib construction.
181. Rear spar.
182. Port wing integral fuel tank bays.
183. Inboard pylon mounting rib.
184. Leading edge bleed air and engine control runs.
185. Weapons bay doors, open (loading) position.
186. Bomb doors, open.
187. Wing mounted cruise missile pylon.
188. Boeing AGM-86B Air Launched Cruise Missiles (ALCM), six per wing pylon, stowed configuration.
189. AGM-86B missile in flight configuration.
190. Retractable engine air intake.
191. Folding wings.
192. AGM-69 SRAM, alternative load.
193. Missile adaptors.
194. Nacelle pylon.
195. Port inboard engine nacelles.
196. Central engine mounting bulkhead/firewall.
197. Bleed air ducting.
198. Generator cooling air ducting.
199. Fuselage bomb mounting cradle.
200. Free-fall 25-megaton nuclear weapons (4).

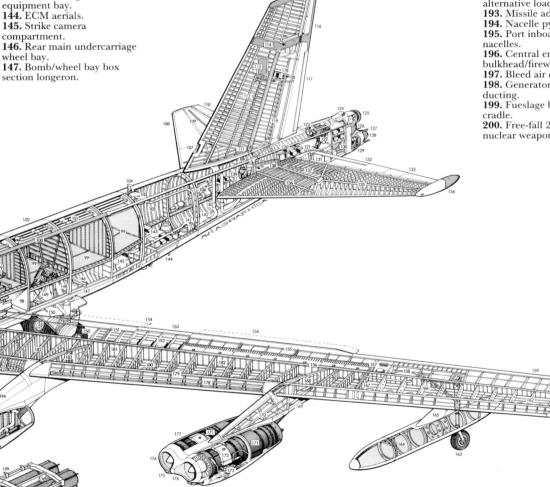

wing was sufficiently thick near the root to house the undercarriage. On the shoulder-wing B-52, of course, this was rendered unnecessary by the selection of a quadricycle-type arrangement for the main gear members, but it was employed to good effect on the 367-80 which led to the hugely successful commercial Model 707 and its basically similar military counterpart, the KC-135 (Boeing 717).

Spanning no less than 185ft (56m), the plank-like wing was immensely strong and surprisingly flexible, static tests demonstrating movement through an almost unbelievable 32ft (9.7m) arc. Wing-droop is always evident when the B-52 is on the ground, but the degree varies according to fuel load. A fully-tanked aircraft rests on its main wheels and outriggers while on one that is empty or only partially fuelled the outriggers will rise clear of the ground. As the B-52 accelerates on take-off and the wing begins to come under load, it will slowly flex and move upwards as if eager to take flight.

Podded engines

Pairs of podded engines were slung beneath and forward of the wing by means of prominent pylons in much the same way as on the B-47 and, once again, these were so positioned as to limit the drag rise at high Mach numbers and alleviate load factors.

Above: A worm's eye view of a B-52D on final approach. The absence of bomb racks beneath the wings would seem to indicate that this particular example of the "Buff" was not engaged in combat when this unusual picture was taken.

In addition, they also served as wing fences and played an important part in delaying the onset of stall. All B-52 models up to and including the G employed conventional Pratt & Whitney J57 turbo-jet engines, this highly successful powerplant "growing" in terms of power output as the B-52 was further developed. Thus, while the YJ57-P-3 of the YB-52 had a maximum dry take-off thrust rating of just 8,700lb (3,946kg), the ultimate J57-P-43W/WA/WB series generated some 11,200lb (5,080kg) dry and 13,750lb (6,237kg) with water-methanol injection, the additional thrust being more than welcome in view of the steadily spiralling gross weight.

The final Stratofortress model was the B-52H, popularly referred to by SAC crews as the "Cadillac", and this employed very different engines, it being one of the first instances of the application of the turbofan. As a result, it was significantly more powerful, each of the eight Pratt & Whitney TF33-P-3s being rated at 17,000lb st (7,711kg st). No less valuable, though, was the TF33's lower specific fuel consumption, which permitted unrefuelled combat radius to rise from the 7,570 nautical miles (14,000km) attained by the B-52G to just over

9,000nm (16,677km), no mean achievement when one considers that it carried exactly the same amount of fuel—47,975 gallons (181,604 litres) to be precise.

Other key features of the wing were the control surfaces—which consisted of ailerons and spoilers—and the Fowler-type flaps. The latter were understandably massive, two segments sliding aft and extending downwards from each wing, there being just two settings available—up or down.

Lateral control

On all models up to and including the B-52F, lateral control was accomplished by both ailerons and spoilers, the ailerons being situated on the trailing edge between the flap sections while the spoilers were located slightly further outboard on the upper surface of the wing. In normal circumstances, differential operation of the ailerons provided sufficient roll control; the additional power necessary during landing, in-flight refuelling and combat manoeuvring came from the spoilers, which could also double as air brakes when operated symmetrically, thereby eliminating the need for a braking parachute.

On both the B-52G and B-52H, however, the ailerons were deleted, lateral control henceforth being accomplished solely by spoiler actuation. Initial experience with this revised system quickly revealed

that a slight nose-up pitching moment usually resulted, while it was not unknown for light buffet to accompany spoiler operation. In the normal course of events, neither posed a serious problem for the pilot. When it came to aerial refuelling, however, the movement in pitch arising from control inputs intended to facilitate station keeping was definitely unwelcome for it could well have had disastrous consequences for both tanker and receiver. As a result, a "fix" was soon developed to eliminate this complication of an always hazardous undertaking.

In the fullness of time, the wing also provided a useful place on which to "hang" other items of equipment. Jettisonable auxiliary fuel tanks soon sprouted outboard of the engine pods. They were initially limited to 1,000gal (3,785 litre) capacity although, with effect from the B-52C, they were much increased in size, being able to contain no less than 3,000 gallons (11,355 litres). This format was retained until the advent of the B-52G which featured smaller, fixed 700gal (2,650 litre) tanks, as did the B-52H.

Armament was also fitted underwing in due course, this invariably being accommodated on hard-

Below: With dummy Skybolt missiles visible in the background and with wing spoilers in the deployed position, the first B-52H rolls out from Boeing's Wichita factory. Variations in skin texture are very apparent on this unpainted machine.

points positioned between the inner engine pod and the fuselage. The first such application comprised the AGM-28 Hound Dog missile, a weapon that remained in use for 15 years until supplanted by Boeing's AGM-69 SRAM (Short-Range Attack Missile). More recently, the Boeing AGM-86B ALCM (Air-Launched Cruise Missile) and the AGM-84 Harpoon anti-ship missile have found their way on to B-52 pylons, which have also been extensively used for the carriage of conventional "iron" bombs, most notably during the course of the Vietnam War. Facilities also exist for the fitment of a hardpoint between the pairs of podded engines on both the B-52G and B-52H, but it is not known precisely what purpose this serves although its small size probably means that it is not weapons-related.

Crew accommodation

Turning to the fuselage, this too changed in no small measure as part of the evolutionary process, the most visible evidence of this centring around crew accommodation which was drastically revised in August 1951, largely as a result of Curtis E. LeMay's insistence. By then construction of both prototypes was well advanced and these duly appeared with a tandem-seating arrangement for the pilot and co-pilot. All subsequent machines conformed to LeMay's preference for side-by-side seating and this

Below: Dominated by a banked array of eight sets of engine condition instruments, B-52G and B-52H cockpits have been considerably updated in the years which have elapsed since they first entered service. Evidence of this process is provided by the two cathode ray tubes, these displaying data originating from the Electro-Optical Viewing System.

had some impact on the physical appearance of the B-52's nose section contours.

Although the B-52 is an exceedingly large aircraft, the crew accommodation is cramped to say the least. On all models, the forward fuselage section features two decks, with the pilot and co-pilot naturally sitting up front on the upper deck on ejection seats which depart upwards through jettisonable panels in the roof.

The navigator and radar navigator are somewhat less fortunate in that they occupy aft-facing and downward-firing ejection seats in an area on the lower deck which is generally referred to as the "black hole". In the event of an emergency on a low-level sortie their chances of survival are not good unless the pilot has the time, presence of mind and sufficient control to roll the aircraft into an angle of bank approaching the 90 degree mark.

The other two crew members occupy stations which differ according to model. On versions up to and including the B-52F, the Electronic Warfare Officer (EWO) worked alone in a cramped cubicle at the right-hand rear side of the upper deck while the gunner sat in splendid isolation in a separate pressurised compartment at the very tail of the aircraft. If for any reason he wished to join his colleagues in the main flight deck area, he would utilise a crawl-way to gain access to the weapons bay which was linked to the flight deck via a small access door on the rear cabin pressure bulkhead. However, since transit from nose to tail or vice-versa required the aircraft to be depressurised, such journeys of exploration were probably discouraged.

On the B-52G/H, the gunner was brought forward into the main cabin area, henceforth working alongside the EWO in aft-facing, upward-firing ejection seats at the very rear of the upper deck. This contributed greatly to the strenuous efforts made to reduce the empty operating weight.

Finally, while discussing crew work stations, mention should be made of the two-man reconnaissance capsule which could be fitted into the bomb bay of the 27 RB-52Bs and all 35 B-52Cs. As far as is known, only brief use was made of this capability but aircraft configured in this way could perform either conventional photographic reconnaissance or electronic "snooping". Nevertheless, it must have taken strong nerves to clamber into what looked like little more than a very large tin can at the start of a mission

which could last 10 hours or more and which would pass in near total isolation; the only means of communication with the rest of the crew was by radio.

Since the primary function of the B-52 was that of bombing—be it with nuclear or conventional ordnance—it follows that the bomb bay was of great importance. Of necessity, it needed to be big, for some of the early nuclear weapons were exceedingly bulky and heavy devices. The bay's large size—it measured no less than 28ft (8.5m) long and 6ft (1.8m) wide—was to prove invaluable when the B-52 was employed for conventional tactical missions in Vietnam.

Quadricycle undercarriage

Scarcely less important in view of the fact that intercontinental range was required was fuel capacity, and virtually all of the fuselage directly aft of the wing served as a fuel tank. The fuselage was also pressed into service to accommodate main undercarriage units, the B-52's distinctive landing gear being subject to such strict security classification when it made its debut that early photographs had this feature airbrushed out.

In technical terms, it is of the quadricycle type, four main members each having two wheels. The wheels themselves actually swivel through close to 90 degrees during the retraction process, those to port folding forwards for stowage while those to starboard fold aft. One particularly interesting feature of the B-52 undercarriage is the cross-wind steering facility. It is possible to dial in up to 20 degrees of offset to either side, enabling the B-52 to fly into

Above: With bomb racks attached and with the weapons bay doors open, B-52D 50679 of the 22nd BW probably saw combat duty in South-East Asia, all but a few examples of the D model being assigned to the 43rd and 307th SWs in 1972.

wind while the wheels are still aligned with the runway. Even more odd, any main undercarriage member may be lowered independently, so if you happen to see a two-wheeled B-52 tooling around, rest assured that you are not going insane. Finally, outrigger wheels positioned just inboard of the auxiliary fuel tanks eliminate the possibility of "dragging" a wing-tip, these folding sideways to lie flat within the wing itself.

One area of the B-52 which was subjected to considerable and clearly visible alteration during the course of production was the vertical tail. Those models up to and including the B-52F may correctly be described as "big-finned birds", the height of the vertical stabiliser being no less than 48ft (14.6m). On the B-52G and B-52H, however, fin height was reduced to 40ft (12.1m) but, regardless of model, the rear of the fin incorporated a near full-length rudder of exceedingly narrow chord. To permit it to fit into a hangar for maintenance, the entire fin folded sideways.

Problems with trimming

The horizontal stabiliser was if anything even more unusual for it was of the fully-variable type, being at the time of its introduction the first ever employed on an aircraft of this size. Needless to say, this caused some problems with regard to trimming the aircraft, for the small elevators were unable to "overpower" the stabiliser, and there is at least one documented instance of a B-52 being destroyed as a result of insufficient care being taken to ensure that the correct amount of trim had been set for take-off.

Moving from the exterior to the interior, the various electronic systems are obviously a key element of the B-52 and it is in precisely this area that the type has perhaps undergone the greatest change over the years since it entered service with SAC.

At the time of its conception, it was the Bomb-Nav system which was probably the single most important element. Inevitably, though, this equipment employed the technology of the time, being typical in that it relied on the use of vacuum tubes and, as a consequence, it was what might fairly be described as "maintenance intensive".

Eventually, age and the non-availability of key elements prompted adoption of a new state-of-the-art digital system which is now in process of being installed in the B-52G and B-52H models as part of the Offensive Avionics Systems (OAS) update. Study into ways and means of improving B-52 capability and survivability began in 1975 with the objective of enhancing the total package, and a prototype OAS-

configured B-52G flew for the first time in September 1980. Radar, computers, weapons control systems, navigation equipment and crew controls and display units have all been vastly improved and fleet-wide modification is continuing, the total cost being expected to approach $2 billion when work is completed in about 1989–90.

Most of the changes associated with OAS are internal, unlike an earlier modification known as the AN/ASQ-151 Electro-Optical Viewing System (EVS). Again confined to the B-52G and B-52H, EVS basically consists of two nose-mounted sensors, comprising a Westinghouse AN/AVQ-22 low-light-level television unit (LLL-TV) to port and a Hughes AN/AAQ-6 forward-looking infra-red set (FLIR) to starboard. Providing the crew with an effective means of accomplishing damage assessment in a "closed-curtain" situation, EVS is also highly beneficial in low-level terrain avoidance flight, informa-

Below: Perhaps the most radical recent updating initiative was aimed at improving the offensive avionics package as fitted to the B-52G and B-52H variants. The new system improves the navigation and weapons delivery accuracy, reduces operational and support costs, and increases reliability. Some idea of the complexity of the project can be gleaned from this drawing.

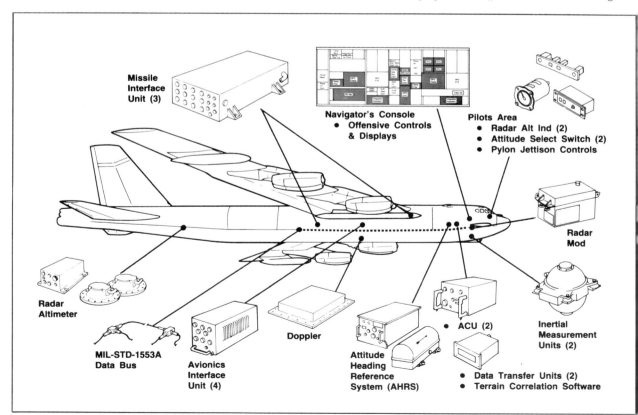

Above: B-52G 80204 was responsible for much of the testing associated with bringing the Boeing-designed Air Launched Cruise Missile from the status of an unproven weapon to that of an operational system. In this view, the aircraft is seen carrying a full underwing load of 12 ALCMs, eventual planning calling for each B-52 to carry eight more missiles internally.

ion presented on the visual display unit (VDU) including radar altitude, indicated airspeed, time to run to target or turn point, artificial horizon and heading error.

Installation of EVS equipment was accomplished between 1971 and 1977 at a cost of about $250 million. Another major improvement taking place at this time concerned defensive avionics systems. Collectively referred to as the Phase VI update and costing a cool $362.5 million, this involved fitment of AN/ALQ-117 countermeasures sets, a Dalmo Victor AN/ALR-46 digital radar warning receiver, the Northrop AN/ALQ-155(V) deception jamming system, a Westinghouse AN/ALQ-153 tail warning radar and AN/ALQ-122 Smart Noise Operation equipment (SNOE) which comprises a sensor-jammer package. Additional AN/ALT-28 jammers were fitted and the number of AN/ALE-20 flares also rose significantly.

Structural strengthening

Modification of the B-52G/H fleet was, however, by no means confined to avionic and electronic systems, it obviously being of little use putting super-sophisticated equipment of this kind into an airframe which was nearing the end of its life. As a result, a considerable amount of structural strengthening took place during the 1960s and 1970s. This work was epitomised by the so-called "Pacer Plank" project which entailed re-winging 80 B-52Ds between 1972 and 1977 at a cost of $219 million. The older D model also benefited from modest improvements in the avionics-related area.

As is readily apparent, the Stratofortress has in certain respects changed almost beyond recognition in the three decades that have passed since it joined SAC and it is this adaptability which has been perhaps its greatest strength. Certainly, there are few other aircraft that have demonstrated anywhere near the same degree of longevity nor many which have the potential to go on and complete 50 years in the front-line inventory.

3

Stratofortress Weapons Systems

DESPITE the fact that the B-52 has been around for more than three decades now, it is only as it has taken on wider conventional warfare applications in more recent years that the range of ordnance with which it can operate has expanded significantly to encompass some of the newer so-called "smart" weapons. Nevertheless, since it is still viewed primarily as a nuclear weapon delivery system, it would seem to be appropriate to examine this type of weaponry first.

At the time it entered service, US air-delivered nuclear weapons were of the gravity type. It was necessary for the B-52 to penetrate to the target area and physically drop the bomb or bombs in order to achieve destruction of its objective. Later, of course, missiles began to emerge as an effective means of

delivery but the gravity device is, by all accounts, still very much a part of today's nuclear weapons inventory.

Unfortunately, in view of the extreme sensitivity which prevails with regard to these fearsome devices SAC is extremely coy about discussing them. As a result, it is difficult to establish which free-fall weapons have formed part of the B-52's arsenal although it seems likely that the Marks 5, 6, 15, 17 36, 39, 41, 53 and 57 were all compatible with the Stratofortress, these varying with regard to size shape and yield.

Below: A typical scene at Andersen AFB, Guam, as a B-52D is armed in preparation for an "Arc Light" conventional bombing sortie over South Vietnam. In the distance another B-52D, returning from combat, deploys its braking parachute.

Above: M117 750lb bombs rain down from a B-52F during the early days of the "Arc Light" campaign. Carrying a total of 21 mission symbols on the forward fuselage, this aircraft also features the hastily applied black underside paint finish.

For instance, the Mk.5 device was slightly over 10ft 8in (3.25m) long, had a diameter of 43.75in (111cm) and tipped the scales at around 3,175lb (1,440kg), yield being a fairly modest 40 to 50 kilotons. In distinct contrast, the Mk.17 was truly massive. Historically significant as being the first air-dropped hydrogen-type bomb to be developed in the USA, it was some 24ft 6in (7.4m) long, had a diameter of 61.3in (155.7cm) and, in loaded condition, weighed no less than 42,000lb (19,050kg) and gave a variable yield in the 10–25 megaton range. Known to have been carried by the B-52, it almost certainly required modification to the bomb-bay doors but it was not destined to remain in service for long, apparently being withdrawn from the inventory in 1957 when smaller weapons became available.

The B-52 is reportedly able to carry a maximum of eight bombs internally, and the four basic types of weapon believed to be in use today are the Mks.28, 43, 61 and 83. However, the past few years have witnessed a change in philosophy: the B-52 is gradually moving from the status of a penetration bomber to that of a stand-off bomber.

Prompted in part by the fact that modern defence networks would undoubtedly take a heavy toll of intruding bombers, the availability of the Air-Launched Cruise Missile (ALCM) has permitted a radical review of tactics to be employed by B-52 crews in the event of nuclear war. At present, it appears that the B-52 would operate in what is generally referred to as a "shoot and penetrate" mode, orbiting outside the boundaries of enemy territory while firing off ALCMs carried on the external stores stations before intruding into enemy airspace to deliver either gravity bombs or Short-Range Attack Missiles (SRAMs) housed in the internal weapons bay. Eventually, though, when the Rockwell B-1B attains full operational capability, the B-52 is expected to operate only in the stand-off mode, with a total of 20 ALCMs.

Hound Dog

The cruise missile/B-52 partnership is by no means a new concept: USAF headquarters issued a requirement on 15 March 1956 for a medium-range air-to-surface weapon to be carried by the B-52. Indeed, the basic thinking behind this requirement was very similar to that which prevails today in that it was expected to fulfil two main functions, namely that of attacking and destroying heavily-defended enemy targets without incurring unacceptable aircraft losses and also assisting US bombers to reach and bomb selected targets by eliminating key elements of the defensive network. While not identical to the "shoot and penetrate" philosophy, it was certainly similar enough in intent to permit the resulting North American GAM-77 Hound Dog (later redesignated AGM-28) to be described as a kind of cruise missile which, once launched, would have proceeded independently to its target.

Committed to production on 16 October 1958, the first missile was accepted by CinCSAC, General Thomas S. Power, at North American's Downey, California, facility on 21 December 1959, and delivered to the 4135th SW at Eglin AFB, Florida, just two days later. That unit had been designated to work in conjunction with the Air Proving Ground on Category III evaluation of the Hound Dog. Highlights of this work occurred on 29 February 1960 when a 4135th SW B-52G performed the first SAC-managed launch, and on 12 April 1960 when another crew launched a missile at the end of a 20-hour captive round-trip flight to the Arctic Circle. These and other trials proved Hound Dog to be a viable system and it soon began to reach operational units. SAC eventually acquired sufficient weapons to equip 29 bomber squadrons operating B-52E, B-52F, B-52G and B-52H models.

Hound Dog was a large weapon, about 43ft (13.1m) long and with a wing span of some 12ft (3.6m). In consequence, each suitably modified B-52 could carry only two of these missiles, one being housed underwing between the inboard engines and the fuselage on each side of the aircraft.

Power was furnished by a single Pratt & Whitney J52-P-3 turbojet engine which enabled it to cruise at speeds of up to Mach 2.1, range capability being a factor of launch and flight altitude and speed. Thus, for example, a Hound Dog launched at high altitude and supersonic speed could put its nuclear warhead on a target as far as 700 miles (1,125km) distant, whereas at low level and subsonic speed range was rather more limited. A self-contained inertial auto-navigational guidance system permitted it to find the target. One particularly novel feature was that the J52 engines could be used to boost B-52 take-off power, it being possible to "top up" the Hound Dog's own tanks once airborne.

As far as the number of missiles deployed was concerned, peak strength was attained in 1963 when SAC had just under 600 on hand. By the end of the 1960s, however, withdrawal of a fairly large number of time-expired aircraft had resulted in a reduction to about 350 missiles. The number thereafter declined steadily to a level of just over 300 in early 1976, during which year it was deleted from the operational inventory, its place having been taken by Boeing's smaller but more accurate SRAM.

Quail and Skybolt

In the intervening period, Hound Dog had constituted the B-52's sole type of missile armament but no review of the Stratofortress saga would be complete without some reference to two other missiles. Both were intended to be used in combat although they would have achieved very different objectives, but in the event only one was destined to be deployed as an operational system.

This was the GAM-72 (later ADM-20) Quail, a diminutive missile which could be carried in the B-52's weapons bay and which acted as a decoy, presenting an identical radar reflection to that of the parent bomber. Since each B-52 could carry up to four Quails, it is clear that in the event of a mass attack air defences could well have been overwhelmed. Certainly, they would have been confused by the sudden appearance of a mass of radar images for they would not have been able to differentiate between which "blip" represented a full-size bomber

Below: The conventional bombing capability of the B-52D model was vastly improved as a result of the so-called "Big Belly" modification programme, which enabled it to carry no fewer than 84 Mk.82 bombs internally.

nd which a decoy. Quail was 3ft (0.9m) high, 13ft (3.9m) long and had a wing span of 5ft 6in (1.67m). t was powered by a single General Electric J85 urbojet and was the brainchild of the McDonnell Aircraft Company. Unlike Hound Dog, it was a very ong time in development; the original requirement merged from SAC in October 1952, and USAF eadquarters directed the Air Research and Development Command (ARDC) to examine whether he concept was feasible. ARDC evidently took its ime over deciding that it was, since it was not until he beginning of February 1956 that McDonnell was hosen to act as prime contractor and almost two nore years were to pass before a production contract vas let on the last day of 1958.

Ultimately, production specimens began to enter ervice with SAC in mid-September 1960. The recibient unit was again the 4135th SW at Eglin and this Iuly attained operational status on 1 February 1961, being the first of 13 squadrons earmarked to utilise he decoy device. Three variants—the ADM-20A, ADM-20B and ADM-20C—are known to have erved with SAC between 1960 and 1978 when Quail vas retired, having never been employed "for real". Naturally, performance capability reflected that of he B-52: speed ranged from Mach 0.6 to Mach 0.9 vhile range was dependent on altitude, varying from 400 miles (643km) at high level to just 39 miles 62.7km) when flying "down amongst the weeds". In oractice, it seems that Quail would have been launched outside enemy radar range, had the need arisen, thereafter accompanying an intruding bomber force to the target area or until such time as it ran out of fuel. Added realism was provided by the fact hat the decoy could be pre-programmed to perform at least two heading changes and one variation in speed.

The second missile which was expected to perform a combat role was the Douglas GAM-87A Skybolt, an air-launched ballistic missile (ALBM) which was eventually cancelled in December 1962, seemingly falling victim to political considerations rather than the purely technical reasons stated at the time. In truth, Skybolt's downfall was the result of a number of factors, rising cost and antipathy on the part of Secretary of Defense Robert McNamara being just two, while there is no doubt that it did suffer a number of embarrassing test failures. Had it attained operational status, though, the plan was for the

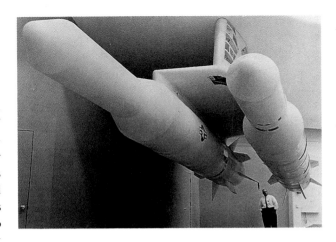

Above: One weapon which failed to attain operational status with the B-52 was the Douglas Skybolt air-launched ballistic missile, cancelled in 1962. This mock-up shows the neat pylon which the B-52 would have used to carry the GAM-87A.

B-52H to operate in "shoot and penetrate" mode, each aircraft carrying a total of four weapons in two pairs on underwing pylons situated inboard of the engine pods. Since Skybolt range was expected to be around 1,000 miles (1,610km) it could have been launched from a position of security well outside an enemy's territory; the parent bomber could then have proceeded to penetrate to deliver gravity weapons contained in the bomb bay.

"Force multiplier"

In the past few years, the term "force multiplier" has come very much into vogue. With the total number of "assets" (in this context, bombers) in decline, it has become desirable to maximise the value of whatever resources are available. The Short-Range Attack Missile (SRAM) is one instance of this objective being attained in handsome style and the Air-Launched Cruise Missile (ALCM) is another, albeit of a different and later generation. Both weapons are Boeing products.

Despite its relatively small size, the AGM-69A SRAM is certainly no lightweight in terms of capability, possessing accuracy and yield characteristics similar to those of the Minuteman III ICBM warhead. The evolutionary process was fairly lengthy, beginning in November 1963 when SAC formally submitted a requirement for a short-range air-to-surface missile to be carried by the B-52G and B-52H. Although conceived initially as a kind of defence-suppression weapon, SRAM evolved into something rather more than that, being capable of employment against soft and medium-hard targets of a strategic nature.

Authorisation to proceed with development of SRAM was received by Boeing on 31 October 1966. Live flight tests began in July 1969 and culminated on 30 June 1970 with Boeing being given the go-ahead to proceed with procurement of tooling and long-lead production items. On 12 January 1971, SRAM was ordered into quantity production; deliveries began on 1 March 1972, to the 42nd BW at Loring AFB, Maine. This unit duly attained operational status with the new weapon in August. The ensuing delivery of no fewer than 1,500 missiles by 30 July 1975 permitted all B-52G and B-52H wings to be equipped as well as both of those which operated the General Dynamics FB-111A.

Powered by a Thiokol restartable solid-fuel two-pulse rocket motor and with a General Precision/Kearfott inertial guidance system, SRAM is 14ft (4.2m) long, 17.5in (44.4cm) in diameter and weighs about 2,230lb (1,010kg). Range capability varies from 30 to 100 miles (48 to 160km) and maximum

speed is about Mach 2.5. Each B-52 may carry as many as 20 SRAMs, eight internally on a rotary launcher plus 12 more externally on two underwing pylons. Fitment of the rotary launcher in the weapons bay naturally compromises gravity weapon payload, but the B-52 may still accommodate up to four free-fall bombs for use against hard targets.

ALCM is a much newer weapon and is still in the process of being deployed, having attained operational status with the 416th BW at Griffiss AFB, New York in December 1982. Initially assigned to those wings which were equipped with the B-52G, it is also destined to be carried by the B-52H model and present planning calls for the procurement of well over 3,000 missiles for use by B-52 and B-1B units. As far as the former type is concerned, aircraft configured for ALCM can currently carry 12 missiles, six being accommodated on special pylons situated beneath each wing in similar fashion to SRAM. Eventually, it is intended to install a rotary

Below: B-52 underwing weapon carriage has always been neat and remarkably clean in aerodynamic terms, this being epitomised by the AGM-69A Short-Range Attack Missile which is depicted here. Up to 20 SRAMs can be carried.

Above: Constant training enables SAC's crews to maintain the high degree of readiness required. Here, personnel of the 28th Bomb Wing at Ellsworth AFB, North Dakota, undertake a routine training mission in a B-52H.

Below: Comparison of this picture of a B-52D cockpit with others showing the later models reveals just how different the layout is in many respects. The unusual headgear worn by the pilot is also of interest.

Below: The SAC badge as applied to B-52D 50677 of the 43rd SW on Guam.

Below: As far as is known, B-52D 50677 of the SW at Andersen was the only example ever to feature a shark-mouth motif. Other colours were standard for this specific model.

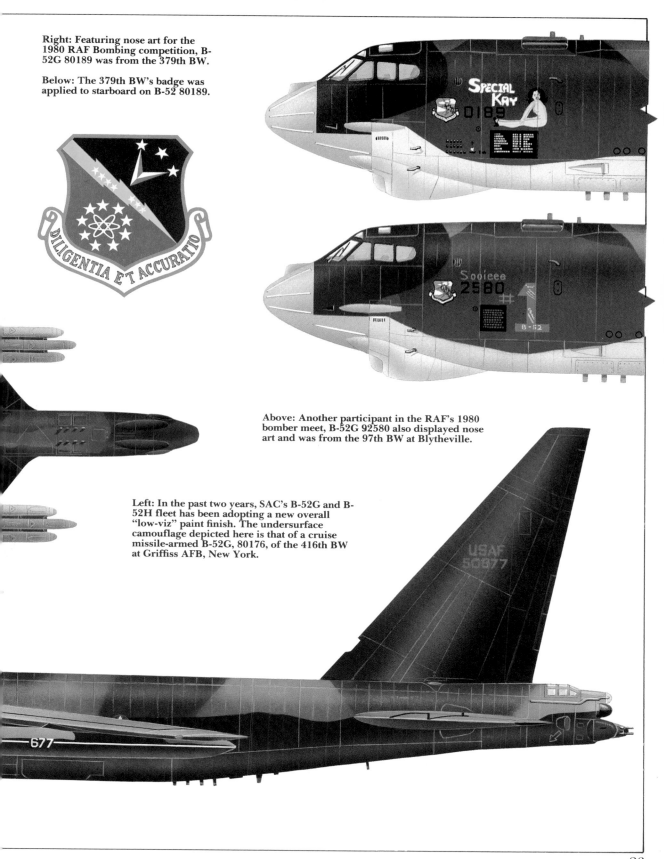

Right: Featuring nose art for the 1980 RAF Bombing competition, B-52G 80189 was from the 379th BW.

Below: The 379th BW's badge was applied to starboard on B-52 80189.

Above: Another participant in the RAF's 1980 bomber meet, B-52G 92580 also displayed nose art and was from the 97th BW at Blytheville.

Left: In the past two years, SAC's B-52G and B-52H fleet has been adopting a new overall "low-viz" paint finish. The undersurface camouflage depicted here is that of a cruise missile-armed B-52G, 80176, of the 416th BW at Griffiss AFB, New York.

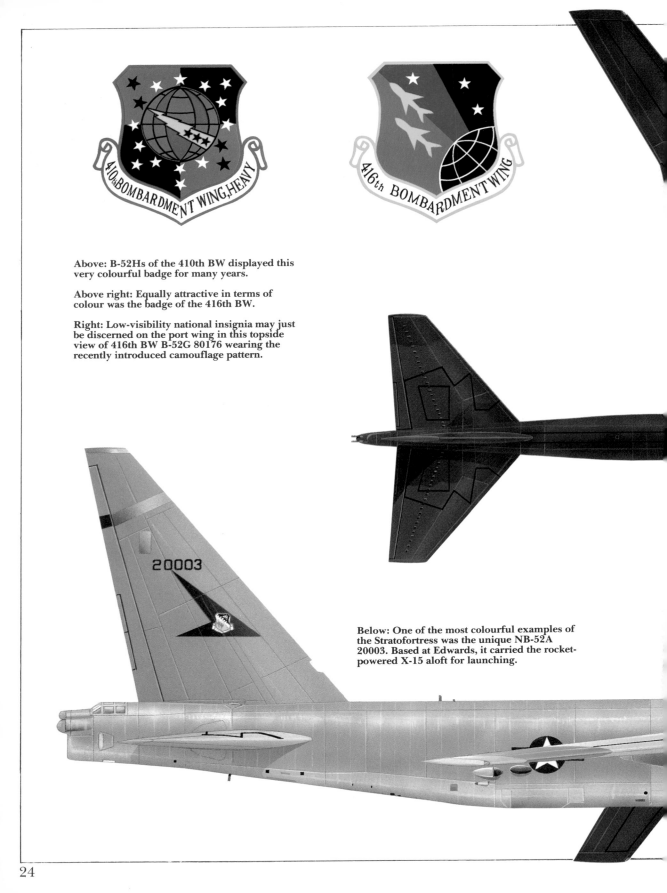

Above: B-52Hs of the 410th BW displayed this very colourful badge for many years.

Above right: Equally attractive in terms of colour was the badge of the 416th BW.

Right: Low-visibility national insignia may just be discerned on the port wing in this topside view of 416th BW B-52G 80176 wearing the recently introduced camouflage pattern.

Below: One of the most colourful examples of the Stratofortress was the unique NB-52A 20003. Based at Edwards, it carried the rocket-powered X-15 aloft for launching.

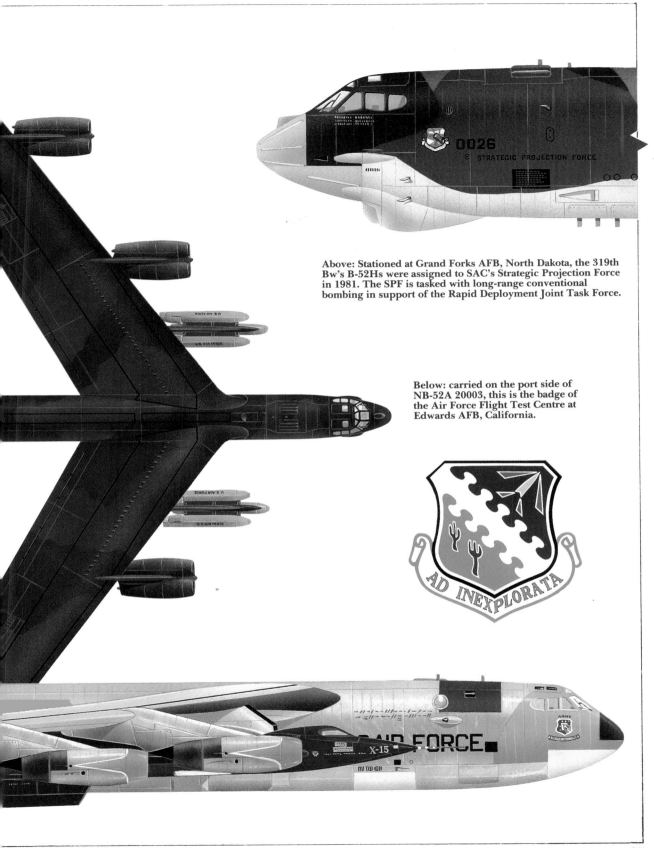

Above: Stationed at Grand Forks AFB, North Dakota, the 319th Bw's B-52Hs were assigned to SAC's Strategic Projection Force in 1981. The SPF is tasked with long-range conventional bombing in support of the Rapid Deployment Joint Task Force.

Below: carried on the port side of NB-52A 20003, this is the badge of the Air Force Flight Test Centre at Edwards AFB, California.

Below: carrying adozen Boeing AGM-86B Air-Launched Cruise Missiles on the underwing stores stations, B-52G 80176 is from the 416th BW and features the most recent colour scheme worn by the Stratofortress: incorporating "low-viz" national insignia, command and unit badges, this made its debut quite recently and has been applied to the B-52G and B-52H.

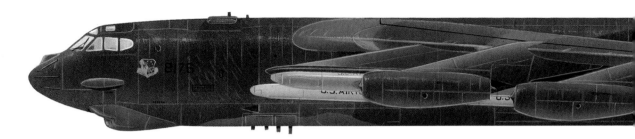

Right: Surmounted by "Red River Raiders" and "319th Bomb Wing" inscriptions, this ferocious drawing of "Yosemite Sam" was displayed on the fin of B-52H 00026 during July 1981.

Below: Artwork applied to 97th BW B-52G 92580 in July 1980 was not confined to the nose, a portrayal of an "Arkansas Razorback" appearing on both sides of the verticle tail.

Below: Also involved in the 1981 RAF Bombing Competition, the 410th BW despatched B-52H 10028 to Marham for this event. Like the other aircraft present, it had special markings, carrying "invasion stripes", the fuselage code "5D-P" and the 644th BS's "winged fist" badge on the nose.

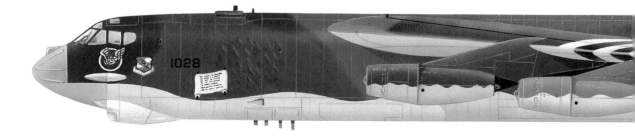

80176

USAF
80189

Right: Harking back to the days of World War II, 379th Bomb Wing B-52G 80189 carried a distinctive "triangle K" marking on its fin for the visit to England in the summer of 1980.

Below: Signifying assignment to the 2nd Air Force, the 17th Bomb Wing decorated B-52H 10040 with this "winged 2" for the 1974 "Giant Voice" SAC bombing and navigation competition.

USAF
10040

USAF
10028

P

Above: Intensive training is by no means confined to aircrew, for SAC's weapons technicians are also regularly called upon to demonstrate that they are "up to speed". Here, a couple of dummy nuclear weapons are manoeuvred into place prior to being loaded aboard a B-52H.

Left: Despite the fact that a considerable amount of effort and expense has been invested in modernising the B-52's avionics suite, the latter still needs constant "tweaking" if it is to perform satisfactorily. These technicians are engaged in working on radar and electro-optical viewing system (EVS) components, themselves forming just a small part of the complex array of electronic "goodies" that are fitted to the Stratofortress.

luncher in the weapons bay and this should permit carriage of eight more ALCMs or a mix of ALCM and SRAM.

ALCM evolution got under way during the 1970s, this weapon beginning life with a very different mission in mind, and making its debut as the Subsonic Cruise Armed Decoy (SCAD). Intended to replace the Quail, SCAD fell by the wayside in June 1973 but research into this project led directly to ALCM-A (military designation AGM-86A). Boeing's initial submission for the cruise missile programme secured an advanced development contract in July 1975. Further development resulted in the appearance of the Extended Range Vehicle (ERV) which made its debut in 1977 and, ultimately, of the ALCM-B which took part in a competitive evaluation with the General Dynamics contender, the AGM-109 Tomahawk, during 1979.

Emerging as the winner, Boeing subsequently received a production contract for an initial batch of 225 missiles at the beginning of May 1980. Funding for close to 1,000 more AGM-86Bs was appropriated in Fiscal Years 1981–82. Procurement has continued

Above: In addition to the 12 weapons carried underwing, suitably configured B-52s may also take a further eight SRAMs on a rotary launcher housed in the bomb bay. Here, an SAC technician checks out the operation of the launcher.

Below: Another aircraft which was closely associated with testing Boeing's ALCM was B-52G 76498, depicted here moments after launching a development missile. The badge of the Air Force Flight Test Center is carried on the fuselage side.

at a rate of about 400 per year since then, with programme cost reaching three billion dollars by FY84. To put this into perspective, this figure represents almost exactly two-thirds of the original cost of the 744 B-52s produced in the 1950s and early 1960s. Of course, subsequent modification has resulted in the amount invested in each Stratofortress rising to quite staggering proportions.

ALCM itself can best be likened to a small aircraft, being stowed with the wings, elevons and vertical tail folded. Once dropped from the parent B-52, wing deployment takes just two seconds. In flight conditions, the AGM-86B spans 12ft (3.6m), is 20ft 9in (6.3m) long and has a body diameter of 24.5in (62.2m). Power is provided by a Williams International Corp F107-WR-100 turbofan engine rated at 600lb st (272kg st) which bestows a speed of around 500mph (800km/h). Maximum range is about 1,550 miles (2,495km), a figure expected to rise by about 10 per cent when the AGM-86C enters service. A single W-80-1 nuclear warhead is carried in the fuselage forward of the wing.

Guidance is initially accomplished inertially, the AGM-86B being "plugged into" the B-52's own system which furnishes updated information at intervals of 60 seconds. Once launched and having made landfall, the Terrain Contour Matching (TERCOM) system takes over. This essentially compares data generated by the on-board radar altimeter with a set of pre-stored terrain "maps" to determine precise

Below: Some idea of the complex nature of the equipment used to load ALCM can be gained from a close study of this picture, which shows weapons specialists of the Griffiss-based 416th Bomb Wing installing a "six-pack" on a B-52G.

positional information. As the AGM-86B progresses toward the target, the stored "maps" cover increasingly smaller areas in greater detail, permitting the degree of error to be "tuned-out" and bestowing near-pinpoint accuracy in the terminal stages of flight.

That is the theory, at least, although concern has been voiced over the possibility of ALCM becoming "lost" in certain situations where terrain profile may be seasonally altered. For instance, lying snow could "confuse" the picture by providing "false" radar altimeter returns, and it is not beyond the realms of possibility that the variations in vegetation state which occur throughout the year could also lead to error.

Moving from nuclear weaponry to more conventional forms of ordnance, the B-52's capability in this area has increased quite significantly in recent years. "Iron" bombs do still feature prominently, though, including the Mk.82 500lb (227kg), Mk.117 750lb (340kg) and Mk.83 1,000lb (454kg) gravity-fall devices. These weapons would most likely be employed in "carpet-type" saturation bombing missions. Where pinpoint accuracy is required, the GBU-15 comes into its own. This is a cruciform-wing glide bomb employing a TV seeker head for guidance, steering commands being relayed by data link. Another version, employing an imaging infra-red seeker head, is under development.

Sophisticated weapon

Looking to the future, the B-52 is also earmarked to carry the General Dynamics AGM-109H Tomahawk medium-range air-to-surface missile for precision attacks against strongly-defended, high-value targets. Trials with this sophisticated weapon began in 1984, the specially-configured B-52G involved in this programme being able to carry four Tomahawks beneath each wing.

In the maritime role—performed by B-52Gs of the 42nd BW and 43rd SW—the principal weapon will be the AGM-84A Harpoon anti-shipping missile which employs active radar homing in the terminal stages of flight and has a range of 75 miles (120km). Other maritime applications include mine-laying and sea surveillance.

No study of the B-52 would be complete without some reference to the tail-mounted gun or guns for, although it is fair to say that the Stratofortress would

rely heavily on deception to mask its approach, it does feature an active defensive capability which could be useful if enemy fighters are obliging enough and unwise enough to engage in attacks from the rear.

On most B-52s, the tail-mounted weaponry consisted of a battery of four 0.50 calibre M3 machine guns, the principal variation in aircraft with this armament concerning the fire control system (FCS). Three B-52As, 17 B/RB-52Bs and all except one B-52C used the A-3A FCS in conjunction with four machine guns. With regard to the other 33 B/RB-52Bs, gun armament and FCS changed, two M-24A-1 20mm cannon being employed in concert with the MD-5 unit, while the last production B-52C married four M3 machine guns with the MD-9 FCS, this combination also being employed by the B-52D, B-52E and B-52F.

On the B-52G, however, the FCS again changed, this time to the AN/ASG-15, and for the ultimate B-52H variant the armament package was drastically revised. To begin with, the now familiar machine guns were dispensed with, their place being taken by a single six-barrelled Vulcan M61 Gatling-type 20mm rotary cannon capable of spewing out shells at a rate of 4,000 rounds per minute. At the same time, the FCS was also updated, the B-52H incorporating AN/ASG-21 equipment which was itself much improved in the early 1980s when modular solid-state systems replaced the original '50s-technology electronics at a cost of close to $60 million.

Below: Apart from the adoption of turbofan engines, the most obvious difference between the B-52G and B-52H concerns the tail-mounted gun armament, the latter model featuring a six-barrelled Vulcan M61 Gatling-type rotary cannon.

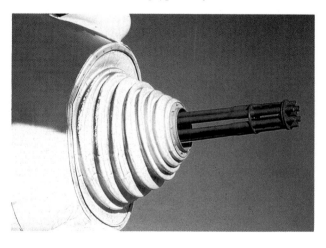

4

Stratofortress in Service

WHEN THE B-52 began to enter service with Strategic Air Command in June 1955, the United States still considered itself to be more or less immune from the threat of nuclear attack although the next few years provided clear indications that this period of security was coming to an end. In view of that, it was fairly obvious that the often large concentrations of bomber and tanker aircraft—some major bases had two fully-fledged Bomb Wings with no fewer than 90 B-47s and 40 KC-97s—would make attractive targets, especially for Intercontinental Ballistic Missiles (ICBMs).

It was against this background that the Stratofortress was produced and, hardly surprisingly, it had a significant impact on the eventual distribution of the huge B-52 fleet, a fleet which at its peak in the early 1960s numbered well in excess of 600 aircraft. Nevertheless, the full extent of the programme had still to be finalised by USAF Headquarters when the 93rd Bomb Wing (BW) at Castle AFB, California, took delivery of its first B-52B in June 1955 and it was not until 1958 that a target of 42 squadrons was decided upon. Each of these squadrons would operate Stratofortresses.

At the same time, it was also decided to initiate a

CONUS STRATOFORTRESS BASES—1955-86

Base	Units
Altus, Ok	11th BW 13/12/57-2/7/68
Amarillo, Tx	4128th SW 20/2/60-1/2/63
	461st BW 1/2/63-25/3/68
Barksdale, La	4238th SW 1/8/58-1/4/63
	2nd BW 1/4/63-date
Beale, Ca	4126th SW 18/1/60-1/2/63
	456th SAW 1/2/63-30/9/75
	17th BW 30/9/75-30/9/76
Bergstrom, Tx	4130th SW 15/1/59-1/9/63
	340th BW 1/9/63-2/10/66
Biggs, Tx	95th BW 1959-25/6/66
Blytheville, Ar	97th BW 1960-date
Carswell, Tx	7th BW 1958-date
	4123rd SW 10/12/57-1/3/59
Castle, Ca	93rd BW 6/55-date
Clinton-Sherman, Ok	4123rd SW 1/3/59-1/2/63
	70th BW 1/2/63-31/12/69
Columbus, Oh	4228th SW 15/6/59-1/2/63
	454th BW 1/2/63-2/7/69
Dow, Me	4038th SW 15/2/60-1/2/63
	397th BW 1//2/63-25/4/68
Dyess, Tx	96th SAW/BW 12/63-1/85
Eglin, Fl	4135th SW 17/6/59-1/2/63
	39th BW 1/2/63-25/6/65
Ellsworth, SD	28th BW 6/57-date
Fairchild, Wa	92nd BW 3/57-date
Glasgow, Mt	4141st SW 1/4/61-1/2/63
	91st BW 1/2/63-25/6/68
Grand Forks, ND	4133rd SW 1/1/62-1/2/63
	319th BW 1/2/63-date
Griffiss, NY	4039th SW 15/10/59-1/2/63
	416th BW 1/2/63-date
Homestead, Fl	19th BW 2/62-25/7/68
Kincheloe, Mi	4239th SW 1/8/61-1/2/63
	449th BW 1/2/63-30/9/77
K.I.Sawyer, Mi	4042nd SW 1/6/61-1/2/63
	410th BW 1/2/63-date
Larson, Wa	4170th SW 1/6/60-1/2/63
	462nd SAW 1/2/63-25/6/66
Loring, Me	42nd BW 6/56-date
March, Ca	22nd BW 9/63-ca 1983
Mather, Ca	4134th SW 1/7/58-1/2/63
	320th BW 1/2/63-date
McCoy, Fl	4047th SW 1/9/61-1/4/63
	306th BW 1/4/63-1/7/74
Minot, ND	4136th SW 15/3/61-1/2/63
	450th BW 1/2/63-25/7/68
	5th BW 25/7/68-date
Pease, NH	509th BW 3/66-11/69
Plattsburgh, NY	380th BW 6/66-1/71
Ramey, PR	72nd BW 8/59-30/6/71
Robins, Ga	4137th SW 1/5/60-1/2/63
	465th BW 1/2/63-25/7/68
	19th BW 25/7/68-1983
Seymour-Johnson, NC	4241st SW 7/59-15/4/63
	68th BW 15/4/63-30/9/82
Sheppard, Tx	4245th SW 1/2/60-1/2/63
	494th BW 1/2/63-2/4/66
Travis, Ca	5th BW 2/59-25/7/68
	4126th SW 1/10/59-18/1/60
Turner, Ga	4138th SW 1/7/59-1/2/63
	484th BW 1/2/63-25/3/67
Walker, NM	6th BW/SAW 12/57-25/1/67
Westover, Ma	99th BW 12/56-31/3/74
	(not operational 30/4/72 onwards)
Wright-Patterson, Oh	4043rd SW 1/6/60-1/2/63
	17th BW 1/2/63-30/9/75
Wurtsmith, Mi	379th BW 9/5/61-date

Left: This unusual underside view of a B-52G in flight would seem to indicate that asymmetric load conditions have little effect on handling qualities, five examples of Boeing's ALCM-B being carried to starboard and only one to port.

major dispersal effort which would have the effect of distributing the B-52 force between 30 or so air bases, a policy which offered a number of benefits, the main one being that it compounded a potential enemy's targeting problems. Less obvious, but no less welcome, was the fact that dispersal permitted the USA to achieve higher levels of retaliatory capability, for it would have enabled more aircraft to get airborne in the limited response time that would be available in the event of a surprise attack.

All that lay in the future, however. When B-52B 52-8711 flew into Castle AFB to join the 93rd BW on 29 June 1955 the first few Wings conformed to existing SAC practice in that they were large organisations. Each controlled three 15-aircraft Bomb Squadrons (BSs) and an associated Air Refueling Squadron (ARS). The latter was initially equipped with the KC-97 Stratofreighter although the more suitable jet-powered KC-135 Stratotanker soon began to supplant it as the primary tanker aircraft assigned to the rapidly increasing number of Stratofortress-equipped Wings.

First operational Wing

The 93rd BW was principally viewed as a training unit—a function it still fulfils today, more than 30 years later—and the distinction of being the first fully-operational Stratofortress Wing went to the 42nd BW at Loring AFB, Maine. This was the first of 10 B-36 units destined to acquire B-52s by the summer of 1959. Receiving its first B-52C in June 1956, the 42nd BW was destined to operate this model only briefly, for it obtained B-52Ds in 1957, passing the B-52Cs on to the 99th BW at Westover from December 1956 onwards.

B-52Ds were also delivered to the 92nd BW at Fairchild (from March 1957) and to the 28th BW at Ellsworth (from June 1957), while the 6th BW at Walker introduced the B-52E to service in December 1957. These six units all began Stratofortress operations in pre-dispersal days and all controlled three squadrons for a time. Thereafter, dispersal became an urgent consideration and the large concentrations of B-52s declined as squadrons were separated from their parent units and reassigned to newly activated Strategic Wings at different bases, a process which was completed in the autumn of 1963.

In the meantime, with the number of aircraft

US-BASED BOEING B-52 UNITS—1955-86

2nd Bomb Wing
  20th BS—1/4/63-25/6/65
  62nd BS—25/6/65-date
  596th BS—15/4/68-date
5th Bomb Wing
  23rd BS—2/59-date
  31st BS—assigned to 5th BW until 1/10/59 and attached 1/10/59-18/1/60, then 4126th BW
6th Bomb Wing/Strategic Aerospace Wing
  24th BS—1957-25/1/67
  39th BS—1957-15/9/63
  40th BS—1957-25/1/67
  4129th CCTS—1/8/59-15/9/63
7th Bomb Wing
  9th BS—1958-25/6/68, 31/12/71-date
  20th BS—25/6/65-date
  98th BS—attached 1-10/12/57, then 4123rd SW
  4018th CCTS—1/4/74-?
11th Bomb Wing/Strategic Aerospace Wing
  26th BS—1958-2/7/68
  42nd BS—1958-1/6/60
  98th BS—assigned but attached to 7th BW in 12/57
17th Bomb Wing
  34th BS—1/2/63-30/9/76
19th Bomb Wing
  28th BS—2/62-1983
22nd Bomb Wing
  2nd BS—15/9/63-ca 1983
  486th BS—2/10/66-1/7/71
28th Bomb Wing
  37th BS—1/7/77-ca 1982
  77th BS—1957-date
  717th BS—1957-1/2/60
  718th BS—1957-20/2/60
39th Bomb Wing
  62nd BS—1/2/63-25/6/65
42nd Bomb Wing
  69th BS—1956-date
  70th BS—1956-25/6/66
  75th BS—1956-15/10/59
68th Bomb Wing
  51st BS—15/4/63-30/9/82
70th Bomb Wing
  6th BS—1/2/63-31/12/69
72nd Bomb Wing
  60th BS—8/59-30/6/71
91st Bomb Wing
  322nd BS—1/2/63-25/6/68
92nd Bomb Wing/Strategic Aerospace Wing/Bomb Wing
  325th BS—1957-date
  326th BS—1957-1/4/61
  327th BS—1957-1/6/60
93rd Bomb Wing
  328th BS—1955-date
  329th BS—1955-30/9/71
  330th BS—1955-15/9/63
  4017th CCTS—1955-date
95th Bomb Wing
  334th BS—1959-25/6/66
96th Bomb Wing/Strategic Aerospace Wing/Bomb Wing
  337th BS—15/9/63-1/85
97th Bomb Wing
  340th BS—1/60-date
99th Bomb Wing
  346th BS—12/56-31/3/74, not operational 4/72 on
  347th BS—12/56-1/9/61
  348th BS—12/56-30/9/73, not operational 4/72 on
306th Bomb Wing
  367th BS—1/4/63-1/7/74, not operational 11/73 on
319th Bomb Wing
  46th BS—1/2/63-date
320th Bomb Wing
  441st BS—1/2/63-date
340th Bomb Wing
  486th BS—1/9/63-2/10/66

379th Bomb Wing
  524th BS—9/5/61-date
380th Strategic Aerospace Wing
  528th BS—6/66-1/71
397th Bomb Wing
  596th BS—1/2/63-25/4/68, detached 1/4/68 on
410th Bomb Wing
  644th BS—1/2/63-date
416th Bomb Wing
  668th BS—1/2/63-date
449th Bomb Wing
  716th BS—1/2/63-30/9/77
450th Bomb Wing
  720th BS—1/2/63-25/7/68
454th Bomb Wing
  736th BS—1/2/63-2/7/69
456th Strategic Aerospace Wing/Bomb Wing
  744th BS—1/2/63-30/9/75
461st Bomb Wing
  764th BS—1/2/63-25/3/68
462nd Strategic Aerospace Wing
  768th BS—1/2/63-25/6/66
465th Bomb Wing
  781st BS—1/2/63-25/7/68
484th Bomb Wing
  824th BS—1/2/63-25/3/67
494th Bomb Wing
  864th BS—1/2/63-2/4/66
509th Bomb Wing
  393rd BS—3/66-11/69
4038th Strategic Wing
  341st BS—2/60-1/2/63
4039th Strategic Wing
  75th BS—1/60-1/2/63
4042nd Strategic Wing
  526th BS—8/61-1/2/63
4043rd Strategic Wing
  42nd BS—6/60-1/2/63
4047th Strategic Wing
  347th BS—9/61-1/4/63
4123rd Strategic Wing
  98th BS—1958-1/2/63
4126th Strategic Wing
  31st BS—1/60-1/2/63
4128th Strategic Wing
  718th BS—2/60-1/2/63
4130th Strategic Wing
  335th BS—1/59-1/9/63
4133rd Strategic Wing
  30th BS—4/62-1/2/63
4134th Strategic Wing
  72nd BS—10/58-1/2/63
4135th Strategic Wing
  301st BS—7/59-1/2/63
4136th Strategic Wing
  525th BS—7/61-1/2/63
4137th Strategic Wing
  342nd BS—8/60-1/2/63
4138th Strategic Wing
  336th BS—7/59-1/2/63
4141st Strategic Wing
  326th BS—4/61-1/2/63
4170th Strategic Wing
  327th BS—6/60-1/2/63
4228th Strategic Wing
  492nd BS—6/59-1/2/63
4238th Strategic Wing
  436th BS—8/58-1/4/63
4239th Strategic Wing
  93rd BS—11/61-1/2/63
4241st Strategic Wing
  73rd BS—7/59-15/4/63
4245th Strategic Wing
  717th BS—2/60-1/2/63

rolling from the two production centres proliferating at a quite remarkable rate, the force expanded rapidly. The B-52 inventory more than doubled in just two years, rising from 243 at the end of 1957 to no fewer than 488 in December 1959. Two new variants had also arrived on the scene, the B-52F making its debut with the 7th BW at Carswell in July 1958 and the B-52G being introduced to service by the Travis-based 5th BW in February 1959.

Both of these Wings had previously operated the B-36, as had three more units which received Boeing's bomber in the 1958–59 timeframe. The first of these was the 11th BW which gained B-52Es at the beginning of 1958 and it was followed by the 72nd (B-52G) and 95th BWs (B52B) in 1959, thus bringing to a close that phase of the re-equipment effort directed at disposing of the B-36.

Attention then turned to three B-47 Stratojet-equipped units, namely the 19th, 97th and 379th BWs which were selected to provide the final nine squadrons of the planned total of 42. The 97th actually led the way, receiving B-52Gs in January 1960 while the 379th BW had the distinction of being the first to operate the turbofan-powered B-52H, taking delivery of its initial aircraft at Wurtsmith, Michigan, on 9 May 1961. The 19th BW followed suit in February 1962 at Homestead, Florida.

In those terms, the re-equipment effort sounds fairly simple but it was in reality rather more complex. The objective to disperse the fleet required vast expenditure on support facilities at more than three dozen air bases in the USA and Puerto Rico, many of which had not previously supported SAC bombers or tankers.

No less complex was the task of selecting units to operate the type. Basically, the 14 Bomb Wings previously mentioned provided the core for dispersal and all of the 42 squadrons which received the B-52 between 1955 and 1962 came from this source. As already noted, six Wings began life with three squadrons. Most, but not all, of these shedded one or two as dispersal became a reality. Thus, taking the Ellsworth-based 28th BW as an example, this initially controlled the 77th, 717th and 718th Bomb Squadrons, operating as a three-squadron Wing until 1 February 1960 when the 15 B-52Ds of the 717th BS split away to join the 4245th Strategic Wing (SW) at Sheppard AFB, Texas. Just under three weeks later, on 20 February, it lost another squadron in the

Above: With refuelling receptacle slipway doors open and the rear starboard main undercarriage unit deployed, a B-52H of the 28th Bomb Wing stabilises in "pre-contact" position before moving closer to take on fuel from a KC-135E.

shape of the 718th BS which took 15 more B-52Ds to Amarillo AFB, Texas, this henceforth being assigned to the 4128th SW. As a result, by the end of February 1960, the 28th BW controlled just one bomb squadron, namely the 77th BS which operated the 15 B-52Ds that remained at Ellsworth. Similarly, the 92nd BW (325/326/327 BS) at Fairchild lost the 326th BS to the 4141st SW at Glasgow, Montana, on 1 April 1961 and the 327th BS to the 4170th SW at Larson, Washington, on 1 June 1960, henceforth retaining only the 325th BS.

With regard to those Wings which converted to the B-52 after January 1958 and which, as a result, never operated as three-squadron Wings, dispersal was accomplished slightly differently in that the squadrons involved were not equipped until after transfer to the new "parent" organisation. Once again, this is perhaps best illustrated by quoting the 97th BW as an example.

This unit had actually taken up residence at Blytheville, Arkansas, in virtually unmanned status during July 1959. Its three squadrons were the 340th, 341st and 342nd and all were non-operational at the time of the move from Biggs AFB, Texas. In the event, the 340th BS was first to regain operational status—on 1 October 1959—although it did not actually begin flying the B-52G until January 1960, thereafter forming the principal tactical element of the 97th BW. The 341st BS continued as part of the 97th in non-operational status until 15 February 1960 when it was reassigned to the 4038th SW at Dow, Maine, where it received the B-52G in May. In much the same way, the 342nd BS remained non-operational until 1 May 1960 when it passed to the control of the 4137th SW at Robins, Georgia, acquiring B-52Gs in August.

The last Stratofortress

Eventually, a total of 22 Strategic Wings came into being in a programme which resulted in the B-52 fleet being distributed between no fewer than 36 air bases by October 1962 when the very last Stratofortress—B-52H 61-40—was delivered to the 4136th SW at Minot AFB, North Dakota. A few months later, in a complex exercise which was aimed at preserving inactive units with distinguished histories, all of the Strategic Wings disappeared along with their constituent B-52 squadrons, their places being taken by newly activated Bomb Wings and Bomb Squadrons.

By way of illustrating this process, the 4135th SW and 301st BS at Eglin were both de-activated on 1 February 1963. B-52G aircraft and personnel previously assigned to these units subsequently reported to the 39th BW and 62nd BS, both of which were created simultaneously at Eglin to fill the gap. Although at first glance looking like a simple redesignation exercise, to draw such a conclusion would be incorrect because USAF lineage follows certain clearly defined lines and there is actually no relationship between the units which stood down and those which were created at this time.

As far as force distribution was concerned, the only other significant event of 1963 related to the

Below: Stripped of all useful components and lying on their bellies, the remnants of SAC's once-proud fleet of B-52Bs forlornly await the attentions of the cutter's torch at Davis-Monthan AFB, Arizona, May 1971.

disappearance of the last two 3-squadron Wings on 15 September, a move which permitted two more single-squadron Wings to begin B-52 operations. At Walker AFB, New Mexico, the 6th BW's 39th BS was de-activated, its 15 B-52E aircraft moving to Dyess AFB, Texas, where they joined the 96th Strategic Aerospace Wing (SAW). The 93rd BW's 330th BS also disappeared, its B-52Bs being turned over to the 22nd BW at nearby March AFB.

Thereafter, the situation remained relatively stable until 1966 when the phase-out of the B-52B resulted in the disappearance of a handful of units and a reshuffle of resources which led to the B-52 being assigned to two "new" Bomb Wings. Once again, the desire to perpetuate historically-significant units seems to have been a factor in what took place at this time and it led to the 380th SAW at Plattsburgh, New York, and the 509th BW at Pease, New Hampshire, beginning what turned out to be a relatively brief association with the Stratofortress.

The former unit received B-52Gs made surplus by the de-activation of the 42nd BW's 70th BS, while the B-52Ds which joined the 509th BW came from the 494th BW/864th BS which both de-activated. Other units which also stood down were the 95th BW/334th BS (B-52B), the 462nd SAW/768th BS (B-52D) and the 340th BW, the latter unit's 486th BS and its 15 B-52Ds actually being reassigned to the control of the 22nd BW which had replaced its B-52Bs with B-52Ds made surplus by the de-activation of the 462nd SAW a few months earlier. In much the same way, de-activation of the Eglin-based 39th BW in June 1965 had not had any effect on the total number of

Above: One of four examples of the Stratofortress which visited RAF Marham, England, in April 1977 in order to take part in the Royal Air Force bombing competition, B-52H 00025 was from the 449th Bomb Wing at Kincheloe AFB, Michigan, a unit which was deactivated just a few months later. Camouflage and markings are typical of SAC B-52s in the 1970s.

squadrons, since that Wing's 62nd BS (B-52G) had merely been reassigned to the 2nd BW at Barksdale.

The total number of aircraft in the inventory began to decline during 1965 when the first examples of the B-52B model were withdrawn from service, aircraft 52-8714 beginning this process on 8 March. Nevertheless, some 600 Stratofortresses remained at the end of 1965, numbers declining only slightly during the next three years, and there were still 579 on hand at the end of 1968. These figures do not include aircraft undergoing overhaul and maintenance with the Air Force Logistics Command.

Consigned to storage

Fairly substantial inroads were made in 1969, however, when a number of time-expired B-52Es and B-52Fs were consigned to storage at Davis-Monthan AFB, Arizona, and by the end of that year the SAC inventory had fallen to just over 500. Withdrawal of the B-52E model continued until mid-March 1970 and there was then a lull of about a year or so until late March 1971 when the B-52C began to leave SAC's ranks. With only about 30 or so aircraft involved, withdrawal of this variant was completed fairly swiftly, 1971 also witnessing the consignment of about 20 more B-52Fs to the "boneyard". As far as SAC was concerned, the total number of B-52s on hand had fallen to 412 by the end of that year, a level that was destined to be maintained for several years.

Withdrawal on a massive scale did not resume until August 1978 but between then and mid-December no fewer than 60 B-52Ds and B-52Fs were despatched to Davis-Monthan where they joined about 150 long-term inmates in a gathering which was probably reminiscent of the scenes at Andersen AFB, Guam, at the time of the Vietnam War's "Linebacker II" bombing campaign.

Thus, by the end of the 1970s, SAC's once huge fleet had been significantly reduced in size although, to be fair, it was still pretty substantial, numbering close to 350 aircraft, comprising about 80 B-52Ds, 170 B-52Gs and just under 100 B-52Hs.

April 1982 marked the beginning of the end for the B-52D variant, for it was in that month that the process of retirement resumed and by mid-1984 virtually all of the surviving "big-finned birds" had winged their way to the storage facility in Arizona, leaving just the B-52G and B-52H to soldier on with SAC. The only examples of the latter two sub-types which have disappeared from the inventory have been those involved in accidents. As a result, slightly more than 250 Stratofortresses remain active today and, despite the fact that some of these aircraft are

older than many of the crews which fly them, they look like forming a key element of the SAC line-up for a good few years yet.

The B-52 has certainly gained "elder statesman" status, being (with Convair's F-106 Delta Dart) easily the oldest USAF combat-rated type, and it is probably fair to say that it has been "at war" more or less continuously since it first entered service way back in 1955. The kind of war referred to is by no means obvious but as SAC's principal bomber aircraft for much of its front-line career, the B-52 has spent many thousands of hours on nuclear alert duty, "cocked" and able to launch at a moment's notice. Even today, at air bases throughout the USA, a sizeable portion of the fleet stands ready day and night, their crews occupying special quarters adjacent to the alert pads which, not surprisingly, are situated close to the end of the runway in order to cut down the time taken to get airborne should the need ever arise.

Less well publicised, but no less interesting, is the fact that for several years in the 1960s a number of B-52s performed airborne alert duty on a round-the-

Below: The six members of a Stratofortress alert duty crew race towards a 319th Bomb Wing B-52H at Grand Forks AFB, North Dakota, in a scene which has been enacted regularly at SAC bases throughout the USA for more than three decades.

clock basis, this concept being evaluated in the latter half of 1958 by the 42nd BW which proved that it was indeed viable. Further trials were undertaken during 1959 and by the end of that year airborne alert was a regular feature of SAC doctrine.

Predating the "Looking Glass" airborne command post by a couple of years, it is believed that the number of aircraft assigned to this type of alert duty never exceeded a dozen, a modest force and one that, by itself, was unlikely to have achieved much. However, had the need arisen, there can be no doubt that SAC was in a position to commit additional resources to airborne alert.

Conflict in South-East Asia

The B-52 did, of course, play a significant and far more visible role in another kind of conflict, being committed to action in Southeast Asia fairly soon after US involvement in the Vietnam War began to escalate. For a type that was viewed by many as being a strategic nuclear bomber, it performed creditably throughout almost a decade of conventional bombing operations.

In fact, only three variants ever undertook combat operations in Southeast Asia, the B-52D, B-52F and B-52G, and it was the B-52F which began SAC's conventional activities on 18 June 1965. On that date, 27 aircraft of the 7th and 320th BWs flew from Guam to deliver a mixture of 750lb (340kg) and 1,000lb (454kg) bombs on a suspected Viet Cong enclave in Binh Duong province which lay to the north of Saigon. This was the first of many thousands of "Arc Light" missions undertaken between then and January 1973.

In truth, that first raid was something of a débâcle, being viewed by many as nothing more than a "splinter misson"—a derogatory term relating to the destruction of nothing more than a few hundred harmless trees—which proved quite costly to the attacking force in that two aircraft were lost as a result of a mid-air collision while en route to the target. Nevertheless, General William Westmoreland, at that time ComUSMACV (Commander, US Military Assistance Command, Vietnam), was reasonably satisfied with the results and expressed his desire for repeated attacks, a desire which was met in abundance in the coming years.

Responsibility for meeting "Arc Light" requirements rested with the B-52F for some ten months or

Below: Combat operations in South-East Asia were almost invariably based on the use of "cells" of three aircraft, this offering the maximum benefits of electronic countermeasures jamming of North Vietnamese SA-2 missile guidance radars.

Above: Conventional bombing activity did not terminate with the cease-fire in Vietnam, as this photograph confirms. It shows a 43rd Strategic Wing B-52D delivering a clutch of "iron bombs" from both the weapons bay and underwing racks and was taken during September 1978 when the Guam-based aircraft took part in an exercise code-named "Giant Thrust II".

so, this model being modified slightly so as to carry an increased ordnance load. Those aircraft engaged in operations from Andersen were able to accommodate a maximum of 27 750lb (340kg) bombs internally plus 24 more on underwing racks positioned inboard of the inner pair of engines.

Even as the B-52F was carrying the war to Southeast Asia, plans were in hand to increase weapons payload significantly and these reached fruition on what became known as the "Big Belly" B-52D. So called since modified aircraft were able to house either 42 750lb (340kg) or 84 500lb (227kg) bombs internally, plus 24 more examples of either type externally, the "Big Belly" modification resulted in a single aircraft being able to deliver an awesome 60,000lb (27,215kg) of ordnance per sortie. Not surprisingly, in view of the fact that the B-52 was now beginning to have a very real impact on the conduct of the air war, it was decided to modify all of the 150 or so surviving B-52Ds to this standard.

Entering combat with the 28th and 484th BWs in the spring of 1966, the B-52D was for the next six years to be the only variant engaged in prosecuting the war effort. During this period, operations were undertaken from a total of three bases and the number of sorties generated could be likened to a kind of barometer of the war, rising and falling in line with key periods of crisis.

Thus, for instance, as the US commitment in-creased, so did the number of sorties staged from Andersen rise from a level of about 300 per month in late 1965 to 800 per month in 1967. Then, the North Vietnamese spring offensive of 1968 and the siege of Khe Sanh saw a further increase to no fewer than 1,800 per month. By then, of course, U-Tapao in Thailand had been home for a number of B-52Ds for some months but it also became necessary to station some examples of the Stratofortress at Kadena, Okinawa. These two bases plus Andersen were kept quite busy for the remainder of the year. Sortie and force levels then declined steadily to a level of about 1,000 per month in the summer of 1971, the 42 aircraft then stationed at U-Tapao with the 307th Strategic Wing being well able to cope.

In early 1972, however, intelligence sources provided incontrovertible evidence that the North Vietnamese were planning to launch a major offensive in the very near future and the number of sorties again began to rise, initially from 1,000 to 1,200 per month and then, in fairly rapid increments, to the staggering total of 3,150 per month, a level that was promulgated in May. At the same time, force levels also rose, augmentation of the B-52 fleet in Southeast

Asia being accomplished under the code name "Bullet Shot".

Initial movements occurred in early February when 29 B-52Ds flew to Andersen and by the end of May no fewer than 200 examples of Boeing's bomber were available for combat duty. By far the greatest concentration was to be found at Andersen which now hosted just over 150 "Buffs", while 50 more were at U-Tapao. Naturally, the B-52D remained in action daily but the B-52G was also present in considerable numbers, roughly two-thirds of the Andersen resources being made up of this derivative.

As far as payload was concerned, the B-52G had not been subjected to the "Big Belly" modification, nor was it able to operate with underwing racks. As a result, it was limited to a maximum of just 27 750lb (340kg) bombs, still a fairly respectable weapons load but by no means so fearsome as that of the B-52D. Nevertheless, the newer G played a full and equal

OVERSEAS BASED UNITS—1964-86	
43rd SW	Andersen AFB, Guam (Used B-52D from 1/7/70 onwards
72nd SW(P)	Andersen AFB, Guam (Used B-52G from 1/6/72 to 15/11/73)
307th SW	U-Tapao RTNAB, Thailand (Used B-52D from 1/4/70 to 30/9/75)
310th SW(P)	U-Tapao RTNAB, Thailand (Used B-52D from 1/6/72 to 1/7/74)
376th SW	Kadena AB, Okinawa (Used B-52D from 1/4/70 to 9/70)
3960th SW	Andersen AFB, Guam (Used B-52 from 4/64 to 1/2/66—TDY aircraft)
4133rd BW(P)	Andersen AFB, Guam (Used B-52F from 1/2/66 to 4/66 and B-52D from 4/66 to 1/7/70)
4252nd SW	Kadena AB, Okinawa (Used B-52D from 1/68 to 1/4/70)
4258th SW	U-Tapao, Thailand (Used B-52D from 4/67 to 1/4/70)

Note: Dates shown in this table relate only to periods when unit operated the B-52. Some were, in fact, in existence for much longer, operating other types like the KC-135A.
Abbreviations: AFB = Air Force Base; BW(P) = Bomb Wing (Provisional); RTNAB = Royal Thai Navy Air Base; SW = Strategic Wing; SW(P) = Strategic Wing (Provisional); TDY = Temporary Duty

Below: Good old-fashioned muscle power was perhaps the most valuable commodity when it came to loading a B-52D with a full bag of bombs, work of this nature being quite literally back-breaking. The wing rack on this B-52D is fully loaded and the weapons specialists have now turned their attentions to preparing ordnance for internal carriage.

part in the remaining year or so of war, being employed repeatedly to strike targets in South and North Vietnam, Laos and Cambodia.

With the benefit of hindsight, it is probably fair to say that the high-water mark in the B-52's conventional bombing career came in the latter half of December 1972, when, virtually single-handedly, it was responsible for bringing about a resumption of peace negotiations in Paris. The catalyst for this was a sustained bombing attack on North Vietnam which went by the code name "Linebacker II" and which entailed no fewer than 729 B-52 sorties in just 11 days of intense activity.

Hanoi and Haiphong bore the brunt of this aerial assault, both cities receiving a battering at the hands of the B-52s. However, the desired objective was not achieved without loss, as some 15 Stratofortresses fell victim to North Vietnamese surface-to-air missiles. It could have been worse, however, defensive electronic countermeasures (DECM) equipment on the B-52 being instrumental in limiting the SAM threat. As a matter of fact, so effective was DECM that the North Vietnamese were reduced to launching missiles in barrage fashion in the hope that this would deter the approaching bombers, an objective which was not achieved.

In the event, approximately 1,000 SAMs were expended during the first few days of "Linebacker II" and the North Vietnamese more or less "ran out", of missiles within a matter of days. This permitted the B-52s to operate secure in the knowledge that they were virtually immune from destruction. At the same time, the threat posed by MiG fighters was slight and as far as is known no B-52 was shot down by one. Indeed, two of the few aerial engagements that did occur resulted in the bomber emerging victorious, with two North Vietnamese MiG-21s falling victim to B-52D tail gunners during the course of "Linebacker II". Naturally, in line with normal policy, both of the B-52s involved in these encounters soon gained "red star" kill markings.

Following resumption of negotiations, a cease-fire agreement was quickly reached and the last B-52 sortie over South Vietnam was staged on 27 January 1973. Bombing of the North had ceased just 12 days earlier, on the 15th. Combat operations did not quite come to a stop, though, for the B-52 continued to strike targets in Laos until mid-April and Cambodia until mid-August.

When bombing of Cambodia eventually ceased on 15 August, B-52s had logged just under 125,000 successful sorties in Southeast Asia, expending the incredible total of 2.63 million tons of ordnance at a cost of 17 aircraft to enemy defences and 12 more to other operational causes. Of the total number of sorties, 55 per cent hit targets in South Vietnam, 27 per cent in Laos, 12 per cent in Cambodia and just six per cent in North Vietnam.

Although once again at peace, the B-52 fleet in the Far East was sustained at a fairly high level until the autumn of 1973 when it began to disperse. Aircraft returned to bases in the USA and quickly resumed the more traditional role of nuclear alert. Henceforth, though, more attention was given to conventional bombing missons. Those Wings operating the remaining B-52Ds were understandably most closely associated with this task since their aircraft could carry the greatest payload.

With the retirement of the B-52D, however, the B-52H has assumed responsibility for this burden.

Below: Although nuclear alert duty is generally performed from well appointed major bases, SAC bombers, like these three B-52Hs, do frequently operate from remote and austere sites with little in the way of specialised support equipment. Training of this kind is of value in conventional warfare and often takes the form of "bare base" exercises.

CURRENT B-52 UNIT ORGANIZATION

2nd BW	**Barksdale AFB, La**
	62nd BS—B-52G
	596th BS—B-52G
5th BW	**Minot AFB, ND**
	23rd BS—B-52H
7th BW	**Carswell AFB, Tx**
	9th BS—B-52H
	20th BS—B-52H
28th BW	**Ellsworth AFB, SD**
	77th BS—B-52H
42nd BW	**Loring AFB, Me**
	69th BS—B-52G
43rd SW	**Andersen AFB, Guam**
	60th BS—B-52G
92nd BW	**Fairchild AFB, Wa**
	325th BS—B-52G
93rd BW	**Castle AFB, Ca**
	328th BS—B-52G
	4017th CCTS—B-52G
97th BW	**Blytheville AFB, Ar**
	340th BS—B-52G
319th BW	**Grand Forks AFB, ND**
	46th BS—B-52G
320th BW	**Mather AFB, Ca**
	441st BS—B-52G
379th BW	**Wurtsmith AFB, Mi**
	524th BS—B-52G
410th BW	**K.I.Sawyer AFB, Mi**
	644th BS—B-52H
416th BW	**Griffiss AFB, NY**
	668th BS—B-52G

Abbreviations: AFB = Air Force Base; BS = Bomb Squadron; BW = Bomb Wing; CCTS = Combat Crew Training Squadron; SW = Strategic Wing.

Aircraft assigned to the Strategic Projection Force (SPF) are configured to take underwing bomb racks similar to those used by the B-52D and B-52F in Vietnam. Other missions have also come the way of the Stratofortress since the end of the Vietnam War, one of the most important being that of maritime surveillance and attack. The B-52Gs assigned to the 42nd BW at Loring and the 43rd SW at Andersen have been modified to take the Harpoon air-to-surface anti-shipping missile.

Nevertheless, despite the fact that both the B-52G and B-52H have picked up new missons in recent years, deterrence is still viewed as being their primary function and all of the dozen or so Wings which still operate Boeing's veteran bomber do constantly maintain a proportion of their aircraft on nuclear alert standby at air bases extending from Andersen in the West to Loring and Griffiss in the East.

Below: In recent years, SAC participation in exercises has been greatly extended in scope, and examples of the B-52 are regularly involved, US-based aircraft often operating from European bases for periods of several weeks. In the Far East, the 43rd SW at Andersen generally supports activity of this kind and was particularly busy during "Team Spirit 85".

5

Stratofortress Colours and Markings

DESPITE the fact that the B-52 has been in service for more than 30 years, colour scheme variations have been surprisingly few, and those which have occurred have evolved largely as a result of tactical considerations arising from changing methods of operation.

Broadly speaking, there have been five basic schemes, including one which was very short-lived and one that was applied only to the B-52D which was, of course, concerned more with conventional bombing operations in the latter stages of its career.

Both prototypes, the three B-52As and all B/RB-52Bs initially appeared in a basically natural metal overall finish, featuring numerous variations in sheen and tint caused by use of different materials in different areas. National insignia in the form of the familiar "star-and-bar" were applied above the port wing, below the starboard wing and on both sides of the after fuselage, while the legend "USAF" was also displayed in "strata blue" above the starboard wing and below the port wing (located between the engine pods in the latter instance). Small "United States Air Force" inscriptions also appeared in blue on both sides of the forward fuselage, while the aircraft's individual serial number was carried on both sides of the fin, again in "strata blue". Other colour variations

Below: Black undersides in conjunction with a natural metal overall finish help to identify this Stratofortress as being one of the B-52Fs which initiated the "Arc Light" bombing campaign, no other "Buffs" being thus marked.

were to be found in the areas covering radar dishes and the like, materials such as fibreglass being painted black, grey or white.

With effect from the B-52C model, new-build aircraft incorporated white undersurfaces and lower fuselage sides, engine pods, pylons and fuel tanks to reflect the heat generated by a nuclear explosion. Other areas of the skin retained a basically natural metal appearance. White anti-flash paint was also applied to the surviving B/RB-52Bs as they underwent overhaul.

Following this change, national insignia were carried only on the upper port wing and aft fuselage sides, while USAF titles were retained on the upper starboard wing. On the forward fuselage the old small service legend gave way to a much larger one—still in "strata blue"—which proclaimed that the particular aircraft concerned belonged to the "US Air Force".

This scheme was successively applied to all subsequent B-52s although there were inevitably some subtle variations, most notably in connection with the white anti-flash paint. For instance, most if not all B-52Gs and B-52Hs featured white areas on the upper forward fuselage in the vicinity of the cockpit section while only the undersides of the engine pods were painted thus. On the final production model it was also not uncommon to see this paint extend around the entire rear fuselage just ahead of the fin and in the vicinity of the horizontal tail.

Star-spangled sash

Turning to unit markings, SAC's star-spangled sash was also a particularly common feature; B-52s which lacked this attractive item of trim were very much in the minority. Again, there were variations in application. B-52Bs originally carried it around the aft fuselage behind the "star and bar" although it was very soon moved to a new location below the cockpit, this being standard on all later aircraft. Unit and Command badges were often applied, that of SAC itself appearing to port with that of the unit to which a particular aircraft was assigned being carried on the starboard side. In practice, although most aircraft were adorned with the SAC badge, it was by no means unknown for the unit badge to be omitted.

While dealing with the basically "silver and white" finish, mention should be made of an unusual

Above: Electro-optical viewing system detail and the location of the SAC badge is evident in this close-up of the nose sections of 28th Bomb Wing B-52s at Ellsworth AFB.

scheme applied to the B-52Fs which were responsible for getting "Arc Light" bombing under way in the summer of 1965. To render them invisible to the naked eye when operating at high altitude, these aircraft quickly donned a coat of black paint on the undersides in place of the more usual white, this being a precursor to the sinister black and camouflage finish of the B-52D which assumed responsibility for "Arc Light" and other conventional bombing tasks in 1966.

By the mid-1960s, of course, high level penetration was no longer the name of the game. It was readily acknowledged that any intruding bomber would have to go in at low level if it was to have a good chance of reaching the target and delivering its nuclear weapons. Low-level training had in fact been a routine feature of SAC training for some time but it seems that little thought was given to developing a more suitable tactical colour scheme until the Vietnam War escalated. Then, in common with many other USAF combat aircraft, the B-52 soon donned camouflage "battle dress" comprising two-tone green and tan upper surfaces with white anti-flash undersides. Large-size national insignia and USAF titles

Above: Resplendent in its pristine finish, B-52D 50087 displays the two-tone green, tan and black camouflage scheme that was a unique feature of this model. Rather unusually, this particular Stratofortress lacks unit insignia.

Below: The addition of individual unit insignia such as the "Arkansas razorback" motif visible on the fin of B-52G 92580 from the 97th Bomb Wing at Blytheville is generally frowned upon, approval only rarely being given by SAC headquarters.

still appeared on the upper wing but the "star and bar" marking on the aft fuselage was much reduced in size.

Serial numbers, too, were smaller and now appeared near the top of the fin, normally being displayed in conjunction with a small "USAF" inscription, and many aircraft carried the "last three" or "last four" on the nose section in black, white or yellow. Initially, command and unit insignia were deleted but these did eventually reappear, admittedly in much reduced size and minus the familiar sash. As before, SAC's badge was usually carried to port with the Wing badge to starboard.

This finish was eventually applied to examples of the B-52C and B-52E to B-52H. The B-52D differed in that, although it had matt two-tone green and tan on top surfaces, the rest of the aircraft to a point high on the fuselage sides and including the vertical tail was gloss black. Serial numbers were displayed in red roughly mid-way up the fin and were often repeated in contracted form on the nose section in red, white or yellow. Unusually, no USAF titles were ever displayed, although B-52Ds were later to be seen with command and unit badges on either side of the nose section. Otherwise, application of national insignia followed the guidelines laid down for the other variants.

Above: The plank-like wing and upper surface camouflage of the Stratofortress can be clearly seen in this view of B-52H 00057 of the 28th Bomb Wing. Other noteworthy features are the distinctive turbofan engines of the H model, the small, fixed, auxiliary fuel tanks employed by both the B-52G and B-52H, and the "window" of the nose-mounted EVS system.

Introduced in the mid-1960s, these basic camouflage colour schemes remained in use until quite recently and, indeed, the black-and-camouflaged B-52Ds were still coloured thus when they were finally consigned to storage in the early 1980s. Since then, however, there has been one further important development in colours and markings, in that B-52Gs and B-52Hs have begun to appear in a particularly drab overall pattern of green (FS34091), olive drab (FS34096) and medium grey (FS36231), more or less unrelieved by unit markings. Aircraft in this finish generally seem to feature low-visibility national insignia, the "star-and-bar" markings being of the "outline" form rather than in full colour as was previously always the case.

Some "hybrid" B-52Gs have also been observed with these colours around the nose section only, the rest of the airframe retaining the standard two-tone green and tan camouflage with white undersides. It is presumed that this is merely a transitional phase and that such aircraft will ultimately be repainted entirely in the new colours.

Above: Believed unique in being the only example of the Stratofortress to employ a white-overall paint scheme, B-52G 80182 operated from Edwards AFB, California, in support of ALCM development for some time during the 1970s. The badges visible on the nose section are those of the Air Force Systems Command and the Air Force Flight Test Center.

APPENDIX I: B-52 STRATOFORTRESS SPECIFICATION DATA
B-52G Model

Powerplant
Eight Pratt & Whitney J57-P-43WB turbojet engines, each rated at 11,200lb (5,081kg) thrust dry or 13,750lb (6,237kg) thrust with water injection

Dimensions
Length:	160ft 10.9in (49.04m)
Height:	40ft 8in (12.40m)
Wing span:	185ft 0in (56.39m)
Wing area:	4,000sq ft (371.60sq m)

Weights
Operating empty:	158,737 to 172,066lb (72,002-78,048kg)
Maximum take-off:	exceeds 488,000lb (221,353kg)
Military load:	(typical) 104,900lb (47,595kg)

Performance
Maximum speed at altitude:	595mph (958km/h)
Cruising speed at altitude:	509mph (819km/h)
Low-altitude penetration speed:	405 to 420mph (652-676km/h)
Service ceiling:	55,000ft (16,765m)
Unrefuelled range:	exceeds 7,500 miles (12,070km)

Armament
Four 0.50-calibre (12.7mm) machine guns in remotely controlled tail barbette. Various combinations of AGM-69A SRAM and/or AGM-86B ALCM carried internally or externally plus free-fall nuclear weapons housed internally. Some aircraft modified for maritime applications with AGM-84 Harpoon air-to-surface anti-shipping missile. Other conventional ordnance which may be carried includes gravity bombs (Mk.82 500lb, M-117 750lb, Mk.83 1,000lb and Mk.84 2,000lb) plus electro-optically guided weapons such as the GBU-15 glide bomb.

APPENDIX II: B-52 PRODUCTION DETAILS

Seattle-built aircraft			**Wichita-built aircraft**			**Variant Totals**	
Model	*Serial Number(s)*	*Quantity*	*Model*	*Serial Number(s)*	*Quantity*	XB-52	1
XB-52	49-230	1	B-52D	55-049/067	19	YB-52	1
YB-52	49-231	1		55-673/680	8	B-52A	3
B-52A	52-001/003	3		56-657/698	42	B-52B	23
B-52B	53-0373/0376	4	B-52E	56-699/712	14	RB-52B	27
	53-0380/0398	19		57-095/138	44	B-52C	35
RB-52B	52-004/013	10	B-52F	57-139/183	45	B-52D	170
	52-8710/8716	7	B-52G	57-6468/6520	53	B-52E	100
	53-0366/0372	7		58-158/258	101	B-52F	89
	53-0377/0379	3		59-2564/2602	39	B-52G	193
B-52C	53-0399/0408	10	B-52H	60-001/062	62	B-52H	102
	54-2664/2688	25		61-001/040	40	**Total**	**744**
B-52D	55-068/117	50					
	56-580/630	51					
B-52E	56-631/656	26					
	57-014/029	16					
B-52F	57-030/073	44					